Remember When

Dedication

Jane, that day, my sister, Debby and I followed you to the UNC hospital, I heard Diamond Rio's song, *One More Day* for the first time. As we drove toward Chapel Hill, I prayed that God would give me one more day with you. Each morning as I greet the new day, I thank God for your presence in my life and then I ask Him to give me – one more day. This book is dedicated to you.

Remember When

A Collection of Articles from one
of New Bern's most popular
Columnists

Skip Crayton

McBryde Publishing
2004

McBryde Publishing
United States of America

Copyright © 2004 by Skip Crayton

First Edition – Second Printing

An application to register this book for cataloging has been submitted to the Library of Congress.
ISBN 0-9758700-0-9

Foreword by N.C. Lieutenant Governor, Beverly Eaves Perdue

Cover design by Bill Benners

Manufactured in the United States of America

Acknowledgements

To thank everyone who has encouraged my writings would be impossible, there are so many of you. But those directly related to this project deserve mentioning.

First to my wife Jane. She has pushed me for years to put together a collection of my articles and it was she who started this whole newspaper thing in the first place. I also have to thank Debbie Davis at the *Trent Woods Times* and Mark McKillup at the *Sun Journal*, respectively my publishers. Bill Benners, my writing partner and good friend, how many times can I thank you? Your wonderful cover design only reflects your artistic genius. I want to thank Arden Lindsay, the third member of our writers group. Also to Jon Segal, president of Freedom Newspapers for helping me place my columns with the *Sun Journal* and for his kind words. To Dana Crayton, Walt and Anna's mom and Frank's wife, thanks for proofing the book. And to my sister Debby Crayton, Jenna's mom, thank you for holding my hand when I needed it the most.

A special thanks goes to both Lt. Governor Beverly Perdue and to my editor, Martha Hall. Bev, we've come a long way from that day on your front porch. Your foreword is so heartfelt. To Martha Hall, TSB. Your infectious laugh and sense of humor can turn a dismal day into sunshine. I like calling you my friend.

And last but not least, to my readers. Thanks for the letters, the phone calls and the e-mails. You are what make writing a newspaper column so rewarding. *Remember When* is for you.

Introduction

For over twelve years, I've spent at least one hour a day writing fiction. My first novel, *Project Twenty-Three*, after over ten re-writes, died for what I call "lack of agent." In reality, however, its death was probably because it was not as good as it could have been, something I now know how to accomplish. The story was also my learning piece – what some may call my elementary education in writing.

My second book, *The Letter Sweater*, was finished last year and now is in the capable hands of my agent, Mike Valentino. We both have good feelings that it will end up with a well-known publisher in the near future. I am currently working on another story presently titled *Jamie's List*. What this all means is that I love to write.

I don't believe in fate. I do believe in God, however, and I believe that He will put us exactly where He wants us to be at the right time. That time came about five years ago. My wife Jane was invited by BB&T to a luncheon honoring women in business in New Bern. Her company, *The Mailbox Lady* is an internet business that sells hand painted mailboxes. At the time internet businesses, especially successful ones were somewhat a curiosity and she was very pleased that she'd been included with those who ran more conventional businesses. God, in His plan, seated Jane next to Debbie Davis, the publisher of *The Trent Woods Times*. Their conversation led to an offer for me to write a column in the monthly newspaper. I chose to write about what it was like to grow it in our wonderful coastal community. The column, "Make a Difference," opened new doors in writing for me.

After three years with the *Times*, opportunity came knocking again, this time from New Bern's daily, the *Sun Journal*. With a circulation over twelve times larger than *The*

Trent Woods Times, I could now reach a much bigger audience and do it twice a month. My column known as "Memories of the Past" appears every other Thursday in the lifestyle section of the paper and is a continuation of nostalgia and a view of New Bern, both past and present, as seen through my eyes.

From the very beginning, positive comments started to flow in. Over the past five years, I have received hundreds of letters, phone calls and e-mails regarding my column. Many of them told me how something I'd written had brought back a forgotten memory – sometimes accompanied by a laugh and other times by a tear. Almost all ended with one question – "When are you going to compile your articles into a book?" For the longest time I shrugged the compliment away.

Again, God has placed me where He wanted me to be. He has shown me that the time is right. And I thank Him. I hope you enjoy the fifty-eight columns that appear in this book. Whether it is your first time reading the articles or you've seen them before, it is my wish that they touch you in a special way.

Skip

Foreword

Skip Crayton's reflections in the *Sun Journal* and *The Trent Woods Times* are part of what makes it so special to live, work or just enjoy being a part of the New Bern, North Carolina community.

His columns capture the spirit of a great small town on the coast of North Carolina – young boys water skiing on the Trent River, dreaming and scheming on Crump's Pond, relaxing on a lazy day just enjoying the Carolina blue sky and dreaming about the future. We all remember, when we're young – the sky is the limit. Every dream can become a reality.

Skip Crayton's columns "Remember When" can't help but bring a smile to you. Some of his columns, like Family Vacations, made me laugh out loud.

Skip's collection of essays brings New Bern of the 50s and 60s to life in a way that you'll want to share and take turns reading out loud to friends and family. It is, as he describes it, a very special place...a product of many things, foremost a willingness to accept and welcome those from other places, people who've fallen in love...with our wonderful community." And he writes his columns with a deep love of family and all the little things that make living in New Bern special, like so many small towns all across the country.

Skip has a special way of describing the hopes and dreams of working together and making a difference. Thank you, Skip, for your beautiful words. The times you write about are a little slower, a little simpler and always a cheerful reflection. <u>Remembering When</u> is not just about New Bern, it's about a way of life many of us dream of. Maybe, just maybe, with this book as an inspiration – folks from all kinds of towns will come to value life in a smaller town where neighbors care and watch out for each other, where kids belong to the entire community, where there is a sense of support for young and old alike in good times and bad – and, there is a special feeling that can only be found in a small town community.

-- NC Lieutenant Governor, Beverly Eaves Perdue

Remember When

Growing up in the '50s

Most of us don't think much about what it was like to grow up in the '50s, but I can tell you for sure that it was a lot different than growing up today – both safer and more dangerous all at the same time.

We learned to ride bikes without training wheels or helmets. Our mothers balanced us by the front steps and told us to push off. After falling 10 to 12 times, luckily without a broken arm or leg, we learned to wobble the two wheels the length of our gravel driveways before falling again. (Stopping was the next thing we had to learn). As soon as the bike was mastered, we ventured into other neighborhoods and eventually into downtown, riding through traffic.

Kids played outside, most of the time until dark, and mom never worried where we might be. A call or whistle from the front door brought us scurrying home. And the things we played with, like Red Ryder B.B guns – I remember being warned over and over not to shoot at birds or squirrels and cautioned that a B.B. could put an eye out. I never knew anyone to kill a bird or a squirrel, nor did I ever hear of someone's eye being put out by an air rifle.

One Christmas I got an archery set. It was made up of a bow and a target, which my father affixed to a bale of hay. The hobby shop sold hunting arrows tipped with four pronged arrowheads sure to bring down a deer or a bear, but as kids, we were only allowed to use the safer target arrows so not to hurt any of our brothers or sisters. One day I shot one straight through my bale of hay. I'm sure glad that I hadn't hit Frank or Debby with that arrow.

We quickly became aware that some of our friends were better at some things than others and learned to accept the fact that someone had to be chosen last for a baseball game. We played ball without head protectors and shared gloves, because not everyone had one. Our left-handed friends had to learn to wear a glove backwards.

Most schools were just a few blocks away and we walked there with our friends, then later rode our bikes. The bicycle racks at Eleanor Marshall School held over 100 bikes yet not a single one had a lock. And, God forbid, if we happened to get in trouble at school. The teachers were never to blame; our punishment would double when we got home.

On Mondays, we had a dollar and a quarter in our pockets to pay for lunch for a whole week and no one stole it from us. From time to time a bully would move into the neighborhood but good guys like Hunt Baxter taught them to leave us alone.

For some reason, the summers seemed milder even though none of us had air conditioning. We swam in a river not a pool, climbed trees, rafted down the drainage ditch that flowed behind our homes, and built camps under newly framed houses. A nickel would buy a Pepsi and another would fill it up with salted peanuts. We jumped up and down as the Dairy Queen truck came by about three each afternoon, its jingling bell echoing for blocks. Another truck we liked to see was the mosquito fogger. The city would send the truck around just before dusk and all the children in the neighborhood would chase it down the street, running and dancing in the blue fog of DDT that followed along behind. No wonder some of us have trouble remembering things.

It was a time when mom was home all day and dinner was at 5 p.m. A time when kids would get together after dinner in someone's front yard and play Simon Says (you forgot to say "May I?") until dark while parents sat on front porches and shelled butter beans and shucked corn. A time when doors were never locked, when baseball was a game and TV was black and white. A time when everyone had a dog and not one had a pedigree.

I guess we grew up in a time and a place where we kind of looked out for each other, there were no pagers or cell phones and dad had the only car. It was a place where neighbors were really neighbors and friends lasted a lifetime. For the most part, we were unsupervised yet one thing kept us out of trouble – our parents taught us the difference between right and wrong. By today's standard we may have been allowed to take more chances. The world has changed and, if I do say so myself, we are all the better for it, but I would not change growing up then in this wonderful place we call New Bern for all the Super Nintendos in the world.

Dancin' to the Blue Notes

Somewhere west of Blizzards Crossroads, between Mount Olive and Warsaw, lies the small town of Faison, North Carolina. I'll admit I could have never found it today without looking it up on a map, but there was a time I could have driven to Faison – a town not much larger than Vanceboro – as easily as I could have found my way to the old Pavilion at Atlantic Beach.

During my freshman and sophomore years in high school, the strangest thing happened on Saturday nights. Kids from all over eastern North Carolina converged on a tobacco warehouse just outside of the town to dance to the music of Ulysses Hardy and the Mighty Blue Notes. During most nights, it seemed like there were three to five-hundred teenagers there to shag on the pine floors, drink a 20-cent draft served up in a paper cup, and check out each other.

The main draw was the Blue Notes, the first live band most of us had ever seen and the only one to play honest to goodness, rhythm and blues – the forerunner to beach music. The lead singer of the band was a black gal by the name of Hattie. She was a combination of Etta James and Elvis. This lady could wail a blues song that would bring tears streaming down your face and gyrate through a rock song that would have made the King jealous. The band had other showmen as well, but the names have wandered away. One guy I do remember was the piano player. I can still see him dangling by his legs from a low rafter and making that keyboard sing while scores of us crowded the stage, cheering him on.

Along with the beer and the music, there was another reason most of us went to the dances at Faison. For my friends and me, it was the girls. We'd ride together, six to a car. I've heard a recent debate that a dress code is needed at some of our area high schools. I can tell you for a fact that would have never been necessary in 1962. We dressed to impress each other. On the way to the dance, the guys rode together inside the car while our starched "madras" shirts rode on hangers in the trunk, so they wouldn't get wrinkled. One particular Saturday night, I fetched my shirt from the boot, carefully stuffed it into my khaki trousers and adjusted the razor sharp creases. After I brushed the dust from my Weejuns, I dropped a fresh pack of Winstons in my shirt pocket and slowly strolled through the front door. Talk about Mister Cool. "Just bring on the girls," I thought. The first person I saw was Jimmy Rideoutt. "Nice looking shirt," he said. "Really goes well with that booger hanging out of your nose."

In those days, dances were over by eleven, especially on Saturday nights. Not only did the kids have to drive fairly long distances but beer could not be sold on Sundays and even in some places, dances weren't allowed. By ten-thirty, the dance floor usually started to thin out, but the parking lot stayed full until after the place closed. In fact, next to that old warehouse, the parking lot remained pretty busy – steamed up windows and mixing drinks took up most of the activity.

Like the crop that supported those warehouses, most have disappeared from the eastern Carolina landscape and I'm certain that the one in Faison is probably gone. Now the bars stay open until two and the kids don't even get started until eleven. The new clubs have high tech sound and video systems. The old building in Faison wasn't even air-conditioned; it was the same for the cars. But some things grew out of those times. I think that the last time I heard the Blue Notes play was right after I graduated from high school. For whatever the reason, they faded away – replaced by bands like the Embers, the Catalinas, the Fabulous Five, and more recently the Band of OZ and the Coastline Band. The shag – now the official dance of South Carolina – spread across the nation and is even being taught in places like Washington, D.C. And the rhythm and blues of the '60s slowly evolved into beach music.

But for me, as I sit on my deck listening to Steve Hardy's Original Beach Party, I can't help but to drift back to a hot Saturday night in a warehouse in Faison, North Carolina. I can still hear Hattie's voice belting out across a wooden floor full of dancing teenagers as she and her mighty Blue Notes helped to launch a new generation.

Halloween

Until my senior year in high school, I spent most of my life growing up at 1800 Lucerne Way. Our house was at the end of the street where Lucerne swept into Tryon Road. Although we shared the same street names as those that flowed through DeGrafenreid Park, one of the more affluent neighborhoods in town, we were on the other side of Chattawka Lane. That's not to say that we were on the other side of the tracks. We were just a little more middle class.

One thing that did bind us all together was Halloween. There were so many kids in the eight or so blocks that formed both neighborhoods that we didn't have to venture into Ghent or Green Park to get our fill of Mary Janes and Tootsie Rolls. Most of our moms were "stay at home" and the thought of a "store bought" costume was out of the question. When darkness fell on October 31st, the streets filled with characters that looked like they stepped from a little theater play. There were ghosts in flowing bed sheets, hoboes with beards, cigar butts, and handkerchief-laden canes thrown over their shoulders, devils with horns made from thread spools, and lots and lots of transvestites. (Why is it that on Halloween, girls like to dress up like guys, and guys like girls? At times the neighborhood looked a lot like Mardi Gras.)

For some reason the nights seemed darker and colder than they do today. One thing is for sure; mom and dad stayed home to dish out the treats while the kids went out, usually under the guidance of an older brother or sister. In a place where doors were never locked, the idea of something bad happening never occurred to anyone.

The treats were usually small, mostly made up of sweets like Tootsie Pops, M&Ms, Bazooka bubble gum (complete with a comic strip), and fireballs. However there were two special people who made special treats only for the neighborhood kids.

Mayor Mack Lupton's house on Queen Anne Lane resembled a castle. Its high-pitched roofs and spires gave it an eerie look on any night but its awesome affect became even more exaggerated on Halloween. But a knock on the door revealed something more inviting. When the door opened, the light from the kitchen flowed into the foyer and the smell of chocolate chip cookies permeated the whole house. Each child was invited into Mrs. Lupton's kitchen and given fresh hot cookies, straight from her oven.

Thelma Smith's mother was a little more discriminating. She had to know you if you were to receive one of her treats. She made "candy apples" and carefully gave them only to those of us who lived nearby. To me that was the best treat of all. It was worth being nice to Thelma for the rest of the year.

Today, I don't hear much about tricks. Everything is treat oriented. But I can tell you that if someone failed to cough up the candy, they usually woke the next morning to a reminder that next year they'd better get with the program. Most tricks were minor, things like soaping car windows or turning over a trash can, but some were more elaborate, like the "doggie doo doo in the bag trick." I never actually saw that one, but rumor had it that one of the teachers from the high school was a recipient. I heard he had quite a mess to clean up.

The only real trick that I can remember taking part in happened on Cleveland Street. James Harold Scott's mother came to the door and offered a group of us one of her biscuits. Offended, we decided that she was going to have to pay. At the time there were about five or six of us but the only names that come to mind are Jimmy Jones, his brother Mike, Leslie Morris, and myself. I'm not exactly sure, but Paul Johnson and Dale Goldman were probably close by. Jimmy sent Mike to the street as a lookout and we removed about 10 or 12 of the bricks from Mrs. Scott's flowerbed. Boy, were we adventuresome.

I guess Halloween has become tamer in the years since the Tryon Road gang roamed the night. But still, seeing the joy it gives the kids, especially the little ones, brings back fond memories of how much fun I had growing up in New Bern. It made a difference in my life.

Drive Ins – A Southern Way of Life

Each town in Eastern North Carolina had one. In Selma, it was the In and Out, Greenville had the original Hardees, in Morehead City they had Dom L's and Kinston had Pharos. Almost all have disappeared, a by-product of franchising. What I'm talking about is the drive-in restaurant.

In New Bern, we had the Parkway. It was owned and operated by Mr. and Mrs. Robert Ipock, Sr., the parents of Trent Woods resident Robert Ipock, who coincidentally owns the Parkway Family Restaurant, a New Bern landmark. The old drive in was located across from the new main fire station on Broad Street.

During my high school years, the Parkway was the center of our social lives. Dates began and ended there. At least some time during a weekend you could find everyone you knew at the Parkway. It was where we all met after the big games to celebrate a victory or mourn a loss. A place we took our dates after the movie, before making a visit to the isolated roads in Country Club Hills. The Parkway was a place where the guys got together after the girls went home to boast or lie or just shoot the breeze. It was the social center of our teenage lives.

In many respects, the Parkway was no different than the drive-ins in other towns. You could pull up, flash your lights, and a carhop named Janie would take your order. A few minutes later, she would reappear with a tray loaded with milk shakes, hot dogs, burgers and fries, along with BLT's, grilled cheese sandwiches and the best fried chicken in town.

The drive-in was also well suited to cruising, a pastime just as popular in New Bern as in larger cities. The two driveways allowed drivers to enter the parking lot, slow cruise past the restaurant, then exit on the western end. Sometimes it seemed like a never-ending train of cars passing by, to see and be seen.

Joe Johnson's dad owned the DeSoto-Plymouth dealership. One night Joe got the key to the gate where his father kept his new cars and drove every one of them through the Parkway parking lot. We thought that was so cool.

On another occasion, a guy named Duke Humphrey decided he wanted to drive his Mercury past the Parkway at one hundred miles an hour. That Friday the word spread through New Bern High, and by the time Duke was ready for his run, the Parkway was full of kids. Duke left the light at Five Points and headed down Broad Street. There were no other stoplights to be negotiated, however there was one just past the Parkway at Fort Totten and Broad, so Duke had to coordinate his timing. Sure enough, when that green Mercury passed the crowd in the parking lot that summer night, Duke was doing one hundred. Horns blew and kids cheered. He made the light with time to spare. What a feat we all thought.

I miss the Parkway drive-in and places like it. I guess it's a part of Americana that's gone along with a simpler time. But what bothers me most is that the young people of today don't have a place like a drive-in for hanging out. A place where you could get a good sandwich and a Pepsi, talk about things that were happening, flirt with a carload of girls, and have some good clean fun. For a lot of us who grew up here in the '50s and '60s, the Parkway, our unofficial gathering place, made a difference.

Summers on the Trent

I've been in love with boats for most of my life. I guess it started the time Earl Williams took me out on his eight-foot duck boat with the five and a half Scott Atwater outboard that wouldn't crank. Even last night when I saw a small Hatteras idling away from the yacht club and smelled her diesel exhaust, the love affair continued. By the time I was eleven, my day dreaming consisted of a Barbour Fourteen with an Evinrude 18. And I'll admit, even today, a Hinkley Bermuda 40 still seeps into my random thoughts.

Boats gave people identity. Walker Hodges had a Wagemaker Wolverine. The boat was made of cold molded plywood in the far away state of Michigan. An Evinrude "Lark" 40, the largest engine in the OMC fleet, powered Walker's boat. I can remember standing on the dock at the Trent Pines Club, green with envy, as he and Johnny Ward skied up and down the river, with what seemed like an endless supply of gasoline.

Another "famous" river rat was a guy by the name of Frankie Spruill, the only son of one of New Bern's first CPAs. I first remember him speeding across the river in a small racing utility called "Jim Dandy to the Rescue." As much havoc as that little boat wreaked, it was not the one that made him "famous." I'll never forget the day he flashed by the country club in his new boat: a 16 foot Yellow Jacket, powered by a Mercury Mark 78a. The sleek design along with the 60-horse power outboard sped Frankie past the marveling crowds at over forty miles an hour. For years, it was the fastest boat on the river.

At the time Barbour Boats and Commodore Boats battled head to head for a share of the local pie as well as a piece of the national market. Each found a spot on the Trent River and both dominated the other manufacturers on any particular Sunday where the river traffic seemed more like Raleigh at rush hour.

The place to be those summer days was the Trent Pines Club. Located on the old Sloan estate, it boasted a huge clubhouse with stay-over facilities, the first and only swimming pool in the area, and a beach club. When Hurricane Donna took out the Dunes Club, the Kinston crowd, drawn by the closeness of the Trent Pines Club, flocked to New Bern every weekend.

But what set the Trent Pines Club apart from its up-river neighbor, New Bern Golf and Country Club, was the new sport of water skiing. Skiing was introduced to the area by a young Marine stationed at nearby Cherry Point, Dick Pope, Jr., whose family owned the fabled Cypress Gardens. He took the club under his wing and within a couple of years started producing water ski shows.

Kids my age and a little older practiced the routines over and over until they got it perfect. I remember sitting on the dock wishing I could be chosen, but age and experience won out. By the end of summer, Pope and Trent Pines owner Wimpy Barwick, put on shows that would rival those anywhere in the country, including Cypress Gardens. There were slalom acts, girls in matching swimsuits with tutus, parading skiers with flying flags, ski jumpers and even pyramids.

One year B.H. Oates was asked to use his custom twin engine Chris Craft speedboat for the finale. Across the river from the club, fourteen skiers entered the water and grabbed towropes. On the beach at the club several thousand spectators groaned as they heard the powerful engines throttle up as all fourteen rose from the water in a sight never before seen on the river and to my recollection never since repeated. As the skiers passed in review, applause and cheers drowned out the roar of the speedboat's mighty engines. No wonder Hank Burns and his sister, when given a choice between joining the Trent Pines Club for the summer or buying a TV, chose the club.

Probably the boat I most remember and the skier it pulled, belonged to Tommy Coleman. I can still hear the rumble of the inboard engine echoing across the calm late afternoon water. As he backed the Barracuda Sportsman out of his Quonset-shaped boathouse, a tall trim girl with a Monroe-like figure strolled down his dock carrying a single ski. Her name was Noni White. Calling for Tommy to hit it, she sprang from the dock to the slalom, barely wetting her white one-piece suit. Watching her was pure athletic poetry as she cut back and forth across the mirror-still river, her shoulder lightly kissing the water with each turn. As much as I loved the water ski shows put on each year at the Trent Pines Club, watching Noni perform behind that Barracuda is a memory that far exceeds any show seen on those late August Sundays.

Swimming Lessons

The girl in front of me was sniffling and the boy in back tried to act brave, but I knew better. I could feel him trembling. For me, I was scared to death. I wondered why we had to suffer so before we could enjoy the summer.

I also wondered how the nice gray haired lady who sang in our church choir could smile, knowing she was dishing out so much pain. Dressed in a starched white uniform, she presided over a carousel of needles dulled by years of cleaning in an antiquated autoclave. That lady grinned constantly as we passed by, almost as if she enjoyed stabbing us in the arm with what felt to me like a dull pencil. Such was the passage of spring into summer. Before we could go swimming, kids had to have typhoid shots.

When I grew up, there was no community swimming pool, no "Y," no "Courts Plus." Swimming was done in the river, namely the Trent. We had no sewer plant and an infamous hog processing plant, better known as a slaughterhouse, was rumored to occasionally let its effluence make its way into the river. Still, I never knew anyone who got sick.

Swimming lessons were a right of passage and were taught by the New Bern recreation center. As soon as we were old enough, our parents would drop us off at the "rec center" where Bill Pierce, the director, would load us into a short, red bus and drive us to the Trent Pines Club where the lessons were taught. Bill Pierce, who died at an early age, was a man much loved by everyone in town. Sometimes I wonder if the constant singing of "100 Bottles of Beer on the Wall" by the kids on our way to and from the club had anything to do with his early demise. Mr. Pierce never seemed to mind, taking it all in stride.

Once at the Trent Pines Club, we were divided into two groups – beginners and intermediates – and marched to two different locations. The beginners started their lessons from a beach, which was really not a beach at all. I can remember as soon as I walked about ten feet from the shore the sand turned to muck. It still gives me the willies thinking about that slim seeping between my toes. The other thing that bothered me was that in the murky "Pepsi"-colored water, there was no way to see the bottom. I often wondered why a fellow stood by on the bank with a shotgun. At first I thought that if we didn't learn to swim, he'd shoot us. Later I found out that he was watching for snakes.

The older swimmers in the intermediate group had it better. M.B. Pope, father of New Bern builder Bill Pope, taught from the dock in front of the clubhouse. He showed us how to dive and do the backstroke and the breaststroke. I couldn't wait to graduate to that group. At least then I wouldn't have to touch the bottom.

Since those days in the early 1950s, a lot has changed. Swimming lessons are taught in pools all over the county, and the river truly is much cleaner, although that gross muck still exists. But one thing is for sure, there are no more typhoid shots. Now the passage into summer is much less painful. This summer, make a difference in a young person's life and take a kid swimming.

See Rock City – Vacations in the Family Car

Summertime is for vacations. It makes sense – school is out and as George Gershwin put it, "the livin' is easy." Today, some of that has changed. It seems that families take vacations at different times of the year and some do it more than once. I called one of my friends last year and was told that he was in Jamaica for his winter vacation. I guess air travel has made it so that if a family wants a time at the beach, they can have it anytime. I can personally testify that there's nothing wrong with Montego Bay in February.

But when I was growing up things were different. Sometime between the last of June and the first of September, my family piled into our station wagon – that's right, station wagon. In those days there was no such thing as a mini van – and off we went. Most of the time we never went to a single location for a week. The better part of the vacation was spent on the road.

One particular trip I remember was to the mountains. To this day I don't understand the pull those rocky slopes have on my generation. Give me the coast anytime. I'm told they have creeks and rivers up there, but if you can't float a boat in it and go to England or New York City, I'm not interested.

Those vacation trips were driven in the family car on two-lane roads. Back then it took almost five hours just to get to Greensboro, where we'd pick up my Aunt Ruth. She came along to help look after my brother and sister and me. My sister, Debby, got to ride up front with mom, and dad and my brother Frank and I shared the back seat with my aunt.

Talk about boring, I've hated to ride in a car ever since. To pass the time away between stops, my parents kept us entertained by playing games. These were games like counting cows, where we teamed up and counted cows on each side of the road. Numbers were doubled when you passed a church on your side or lost when you passed a cemetery. Another game, similar in nature was Fords and Chevrolets, a game my friend Louise Jones used to love to play.

Lunch was a real occasion while traveling along the major two lane routes. There were no fast food joints along the way. No Mickie D's or KFC's, and on the type of budget we used for travel, we'd have never stopped anyway. Usually at 11:45, we'd all start looking for a "Roadside Table" conveniently placed beside the highway by the Department of Transportation so that gypsy families like ours could find a place to eat. It was apparent that many others traveled as frugally as we did, as there were times we drove until after 1 p.m. before we found a vacant table.

Lunch was also an adventure. While dad hauled the cooler from the back of the wagon, the rest of us set the table, shooing away regiments of flies standing by for their next feeding. Our feast was made up of baloney and cheese sandwiches, crackers and potted meat – a canned product somewhat akin to Spam – and Duke's Relish sandwiches. (This product, is made by combining Duke's mayonnaise with pickle relish, and is – I kid you not – still available in most grocery stores.) The meal was washed down by a tasty concoction called bug juice, a beverage somewhat related to Koolaid. Cokes and Pepsis were a treat held for the afternoon break.

After lunch it was off again down the road to places like Blowing Rock, Mystery Village, Luray Caverns, Ruby Falls, and Chimney Rock, where it was advertised that you could see five states from its pinnacle. Another place of interest was called "Rock City." Located somewhere between the North Carolina and Tennessee border, it was a must see. It had to be. Every single barn and outhouse between Greensboro and the state line had its advertisement painted on its roof. By the end of the day, everyone in traffic could tell where we'd been. All they had to do is check out the bumper stickers the various places of interest had applied to the back of our car.

Today when we travel, I always have a reservation for a place to stay, but in 1955...Noooo. There were times when we drove around until ten or eleven o'clock at night looking for a "Quality Court" that didn't have a "No Vacancy" sign blinking by the front door. Most of those nights, while my dad searched for a "clean" motel, I was forced to find a place to sleep on the floor in the backseat. I learned to get used to the hump while my younger brother nestled his head in my aunt's lap.

And to find a motel with a pool? That was an unexpected thrill. One thing I do miss about those old motor courts and motels is the vibrating bed. For a quarter, you could get ten to fifteen minutes of relaxation as the bed shook back and forth. I can still remember lying on the bed hoping that it would never stop only to be disappointed when it did. How a box of quarters would have cured that empty feeling.

We've come a long way from the days of the late '50s. Gone are most of the main two lane routes where the poetry of a Burma Shave sign has been replaced by six lanes of white-knuckle traffic. Gone are the mom and pop service stations where an ice cold Pepsi waited inside along with a pack of Nabs. And for the most part, gone are the family units that journeyed the highways for days on end, spending time together while school was out. As much as I hate riding in a car, I miss those family trips. The trips that taught us to get along with each other a little better and to make a difference in each others' lives.

Barbour Boats

When I was about ten years old, I accompanied my father to the country club on a Saturday afternoon that was to change my life.

Dad was going to play golf and it was going to be my job to entertain myself playing around the club. After he teed off, I ran into my friend Earl Williams who introduced me to what would develop into a love affair that has lasted a lifetime. No, it wasn't my wife Jane, I hadn't met her yet.

Earl showed me his new boat. He had a Barbour twelve footer with an eighteen horse Evinrude on the back. It was the neatest thing I'd ever seen, and at ten, his father let him take it out by himself.

That afternoon, I had more fun than I'd ever had in my life. I was totally shocked at my father's reaction to the fact that I'd been boating with my friend Earl. I saw no danger in it then – nor do I today – but my father was angry that I'd used such poor judgment and could have fallen over and drowned while he played golf. He said my mom would never have forgiven him if that had happened.

I guess my father's reaction made the mystique of boating even that more exciting and I couldn't get enough. One thing I learned, however, was to never again volunteer information when I went out on my friends' boats.

Back in 1956, boats were built of wood. No one had ever heard of fiberglass and no one really cared. The best boats in the world were built right here in New Bern by Barbour Boat Works and came in sizes from twelve feet to twenty six, if you don't include the forty foot flagship, "Stardust," but that's a different story all in itself.

The boats had lapstraked hulls, painted in mostly pastel colors with decks and interiors of highly varnished mahogany.

The cleats and other hardware were bright chrome and polished brass. The vast majority of those vessels were powered by outboard engines; however there was the occasional inboard and the revolutionary inboard/outboard engines.

I used to go to the docks at the country club or the Trent Pines Club to see the Barbours and wish. If wishing could have gotten me a Barbour outboard, I'd have had over thirty by the time I was eleven. I remember placing a tooth under my pillow, hoping to wake the next morning and find that the tooth fairy had left a sixteen-foot Silver Clipper.

When fiberglass replaced wood as the primary material for boats, Barbour, like so many other famous boat companies that didn't make the transition, eventually went out of business. Soon the dominance the company had on the Trent River gave way to Robalo, Mako, Parker, and others. Only a few Barbours still exist. One that comes to mind belongs to Ken McCotter. It was his boat growing up and he has just had it refinished to its original luster. I'm sure he'd be proud to show it to anyone.

The Barbour plant where the boats were built has recently been torn down, making way for more progress in downtown. Until recently, the last three company owned boats sat in the show room on South Front Street. Those boats seemed to be locked in time, displayed in a window time had forgotten. Thanks to the Rivenbark family, who owned Barbour Boat Works, the last remaining boats, still in factory condition, have been saved. They, along with the "Stardust," are all on permanent loan to the North Carolina Maritime Museum in Beaufort where we can all enjoy that part of our past. Barbour Boats introduced me to a passion that has lasted a lifetime. Boating has taken me from Annapolis to Miami and from Morehead City to Bermuda. To this writer, the joy and excitement of being on the water has really made a difference.

Crump's Pond

As I leaned my bike against the tree, I could tell they were already onboard. Their laughter gave them away. I made my way down the hill to the dock where the *Pursuit*, Scrappy Bell Sr.'s thirty-foot sloop sat in her berth, her bow pointed downriver. Aboard were Jim Bryan and George Bell.

The *Pursuit* was a kind of clubhouse to us. It was where we met on Saturday mornings, before starting our day on the river. She had been built in Elizabeth City in 1939 and was the first of many sailboats I'd step aboard in my lifetime. Below the boat was warm colored wood with a galley, a settee and bunks. She also held hidden cargo, our stash of men's magazines, those with names like *Esquire*, *Argosy*, *Duke* and *Gent* — magazines whose centerfolds wore more clothes than those found on the covers of today's *People* and *Cosmopolitan*.

But this day we weren't there to look at pictures. This day we were going diving. To us diving was not with tanks but what today we call snorkeling. When I joined Jim and George below, they were checking out their fins, masks and snorkels. This was serious business.

When we were ready, we jumped overboard and swam next door to a place we called "Stevens' Beach." The beach was one of only a few stretches of sandy shore on the Trent River. We found it a good place to practice, but once in the water, the visibility dropped to two or three inches. The tannins in the river made it more like swimming in a lake of Pepsi Cola. There had to be a better place.

The next Saturday, George and Jim were waiting for me on the dock. Anxiously George said, "Man, I've found the place."

"Where?" I asked.

"Right over there." George pointed across the river to a small spillway and bridge that sat next to the Crump farm mansion. "The pond's so clear, it looks just like Silver Springs in Florida."

Moments later we pulled the Bell's duck boat ashore at the Crump house and walked up to the veranda. Sitting in his green rocker was Mr. Crump. "How you boys doing?" he asked.

We exchanged greetings then George asked him if we could dive in his pond. "Not a problem," he said, "But you'll have to leave that in the boat. I don't want anybody shooting my fish." What Mr. Crump was referring to was Jim's spear gun.

After Jim stowed the gun back in the boat, he joined George and me in the water. The pond was about ten acres in size and was fed by artesian wells. The concrete dam and spillway kept the river at bay and George was right, it was so clear you could see the bottom, some twenty feet down. Kelp-like vegetation grew up from the floor of the pond and created tunnels which we found to be the hiding place for hundreds of fish. We decided that there had to be a way to smuggle in the spear gun.

The next Saturday, Jim played frogman. We let him off in the middle of the river and he slowly stole up to the spillway and placed the gun on the other side. Afterward, we picked him up, beached the boat, paid our respects to Mr. Crump and jumped into the pond. Within minutes, Jim was shooting fish. Our plan was to reverse the action as soon as we'd shot enough fish for supper, then pick up our catch on other side of the spillway. What we didn't count on was the clarity of the water. After the third fish had been bagged, I heard a slapping sound. When I looked up Mr. Crump was beating the water with a paddle. He'd been watching us all along.

The next few Saturdays were dismal. We could see the pond from across the river, but it was now out of bounds. "I've got an idea," Jim said. "Why don't we ask Mr. Hanes if we could go in from his side?" The pond was the dividing line between the Crump farm and the Hanes farm.

"Let's give it a try," I said.

Later that day, we told Mr. Hanes our story. A man of few words but hardy determination, Mr. Hanes told us to stay right where we were and he'd take care of everything. A few minutes later he appeared with a large gray stick in his hand. Attached to the stick was a three-foot fuse, its end popping and burning like a sparkler. "You boys come with me," he said.

We walked with Mr. Hanes to the edge of the pond. Just on the other side I could see Mr. Crump in his green rocker.

"You tell these boys they can't swim in the pond?" Hanes yelled.

"Not if they're going to shoot my fish," Crump called back.

"Pond's half mine, ain't it." The fuse burned shorter.

"That doesn't matter." Crump got out of his rocker.

"If the pond's half mine then so are the fish," Hanes shouted back.

"I won't have them shooting the fish."

"Fine with me," Hanes said. The fuse burned closer to the stick. "I'll just blow up the spillway."

Crump didn't answer at first. He knew Hanes would do just what he'd said. As we waited for the answer, the fuse got shorter and shorter. "Okay, they can swim in the pond." Crump gave in. "But they'll have to go in on your side."

Hanes raised his left hand in acknowledgment then turned. "You heard him boys. Go get your stuff."

As we walled back toward Mr. Hanes' house I looked at him. The fuse was now about two inches from the large gray stick. "Is that really dynamite?" I asked.

"You bet your sweet....." I never heard the last word which I'm sure had something to do with my hind parts. It was covered up by the hissing sound made when Mr. Hanes wet his thumb and index finder and snuffed out the fire at the end of the fuse.

Boy, growing up New Bern was a lot of fun. That day, Mr. Hanes really made a difference.

Saturday Night at the Movies

I plopped two quarters down and the lady handed me two tickets. She told me that the movie had already started, but we didn't care. After a stop at the concession stand where I bought a box of popcorn for my date, two Pepsis and a box of Goobers, we found a seat to watch Frankie Avalon and Annette "Funnybelly" cavort through another "Beach Blanket" movie. It was Saturday night at the movies, all for under a dollar.

Instead of multiplexes, movies were shown in buildings called theaters, complete with stages and in many cases ornate proscenium arches adorned with Gothic figures and flowing drapes that parted as the movie began. In some cities, they rivaled Broadway theaters. The Carolina in Greensboro kept its pipe organ, left over from the days of silent films and used it to entertain the audience before the start of the show.

Things were similar in New Bern without the ornate trappings. We had three theaters. The Kehoe (later to be renamed the Tryon) occupied the space now serving as the Saax Bradbury Playhouse. The Colonial was just up Pollock on the opposite side of the street and is now Branch's Office Supply. The third one, The Masonic, was across from Central School, and although now closed, is still a theater. (At one time it was said to be the longest continuously running movie theater in the country.)

When I was in grade school, the movies were a great entertainment for the kids in the neighborhood. What we saw on Saturday mornings was different from what was shown at night. The flicks were called "Kiddie Shows" and featured mostly westerns with stars like Roy Rogers and Dale Evans, Whip Wilson, Lash LaRue and Hopalong Cassidy. Along with those double features, there were usually four or five cartoons and at least two serials – Dick Tracy was my favorite.

As we got older and discovered the opposite sex, the movies served another purpose. Since Friday nights were taken up with football and basketball games, Saturday nights became movie nights. I guess my favorite theater was the Masonic. It was always clean and usually offered first run pictures. The theater was operated by an affable fellow by the name of "Shorty" Kafer (One of the 2003 inductees into the New Bern High School Athletic Hall of Fame.) I believe Shorty knew everyone in town. One of his best tricks was to fire up his popcorn maker midway through the film so that the smell would permeate the theater and create an unbearable craving for more popcorn, chased by a large Pepsi.

After the movie, it was a stop by the Parkway for a burger followed by a trip to some romantic place for what our parents called "necking." It didn't take any of us long to find out there was a place where we could combine all three – movies, burgers, and a little "making out."

The Midway drive-in theater was located just across the Trent River in James City. It was owned and operated by two of the hardest working people I've ever known: Gordon and Hazel Parrott. They started their day at five in the morning with breakfast at Warner's Cafe on South Front Street. Then it was off to Gordon's Food Center for the rest of the day. As soon as the grocery store closed, the drive-in opened.

A trip to the drive-in was an all evening affair. Teenagers double-dated in cars with steamed up windows right next to a family with three kids asleep in the back seat. Other couples pulled in, hung the speaker on the window, then let three or more freeloaders out of the trunk.

At the break between shows, the trek from the car to the snack bar began. Along with popcorn, they also sold burgers, hot dogs, fries and shakes. Most, however, had to be back in their cars in time to play LUCKY, a bingo-type game called by Hazel herself. Honking horns identified the winners.

With dying downtowns, movies had to find a way not only to survive but also to flourish. That's what gave way to the multiplexes. What happened to the drive-ins is still a mystery to me, but for some reason I miss them most of all. There was just nothing like impressing that first date by driving off with the speaker still attached to the window.

Editor's Note

Restoration of the Masonic Theater has now been completed and it is occasionally open to the public for live theater productions.

Bill Jefferay – Radio Pioneer

"God bless us everyone," I said, as the director signaled a wrap. The year was 1950 and those words were my only lines. The place was the production studio at WHIT radio. We had just finished taping a presentation of the Dickens classic, *A Christmas Carol*, which was scheduled to be aired on Christmas Eve. My father played Bob Cratchet to Colonel Albert Willis' Scrooge and at the age of five, I made my one and only venture into acting as Tiny Tim.

For most of the 20th century, radio had been king. The formats were mixed between live, recorded and network shows. Programs like "Amos and Andy," "Jack Benny" and "Fibber McGee and Molly" dominated the evening broadcast. Music brought directly from the Blue Room of the Roosevelt Hotel in downtown New Orleans placed the listener right in front of a live performance of a named Big Band. And Saturday mornings excited the kids with stories from "The Lone Ranger" to "Sky King" to "Hopalong Cassidy."

The WHIT studio was state of the art and mirrored many of the national studios with production staff and live "On Air" presentations. Affiliated with such networks as The Mutual Broadcasting System and the Tobacco Radio Network, the station aired nightly news programs with famous "Commentators" like Gabriel Heater, whose trademark "AH, there's good news tonight" kicked off his show.

But the winds of change were looming on the horizon. On December 22, 1953, a small CBS affiliate located at the end of Evans Street extension in Greenville, turned on its transmitter and started sending its signal "From the Capital to the Coast." Along with sound, however, it sent pictures. WNCT, eastern North Carolina's first television station, had been born.

For the first time, the baby boomers could place faces to all the familiar names on Saturday morning. Television not only stole radio's format, it made it better. The technology generation found it easy to turn to the new medium. Many smelled the doom of radio. But that was also going to change.

"Oh, it's so beautiful," the wife said to her husband as they approached the foot of the Neuse River Bridge. "Let's stop for just a moment and take it all in." Just ahead, across the mile wide span, New Bern twinkled, its lights reflecting against the river. The spires and towers lit the late November night crowned by the Christmas lights that outlined the water tower. It was her first look at the town that was to become her new home and she loved what she saw.

They sat there for a moment absorbed in thoughts about the future then the husband checked his three sleeping children tucked in the back seat then pulled his Buick back onto the bridge. That night in 1958 radio was about to change, not just for New Bern but for North Carolina. The visionary driving that car was Bill Jefferay. Along with his wife Audrey and their three children, they'd left Saint Louis for a new home in New Bern. He'd bought WRNB radio and was going to make it the first all "Rock and Roll" station in all of North Carolina.

From the beginning, the all-rock format captured the kids of my generation. Instead of listening to an hour or two of popular music, generally followed by snide remarks from a broadcaster still lost in the big band era, we could listen to our music all day long. WRNB's airwaves were full of people like Bill Haley and the Comets, The Platters, Little Richard, and, of course, Elvis. The 45-rpm records, with the big hole in the middle, were spun by live personalities who loved the music and connected with their audiences. They were no longer broadcasters. They were disc jockeys.

Jefferay and his family quickly settled into the community and became very active citizens. They were involved in church, the chamber and especially the schools. Jefferay started covering New Bern High School football, bringing those same personalities that we looked up to right to our campus for the games.

One of his best finds was a man named George Nelson. Soon after he opened WRNB, Nelson approached Jefferay and was hired on the spot. Shortly Nelson became the station's general manager. His morning drive show, sometimes controversial yet always entertaining became legendary, setting the example for people like Don Imus.

Before long, Bill Jefferay became known as the dean of the rock format. The success of his station reached all across the state. Even the fabled WKIX in Raleigh paid Jefferay a visit and asked to copy his programming.

And who could forget, "Music 'til Midnight," a romantic combination that started at ten on Saturday nights and ended when the station signed off. I wonder how many of us fell in love with the sound of Johnny Mathis, cooing from the single speaker as we parked in the family car somewhere in the Trent Woods area. (I always pondered who added the word "Trent.")

The WRNB call sign does not reside in New Bern anymore. Its 1490 place on the AM dial is still here as WWNB, a talk format. As things changed in the '50s, they changed again for music stations with the rise of tall FM towers, but one thing is for sure. Bill Jefferay was right. Popular music is still one of the strongest formats in radio.

A few years ago the Jefferays moved to Raleigh where they are enjoying an active retirement. But there is one more thing that is for sure, Bill Jefferay was a radio pioneer and his impact had as much an affect on our community as any other person at the time. He really made a difference.

If She Doesn't Remember Howdy Doody, Don't Ask Her Out

The first television set I ever remember seeing belonged to Junius Johnson. On weekday afternoons, I joined his son Paul, Paul's sisters Betsy and Peggy and half the other kids in the neighborhood to watch Howdy Doody on a snowy nine-inch screen. The picture was broadcast all the way from Norfolk, Virginia. Even compared to today's high definition TV, it was a real adventure.

I like to compare Junius to the Jim O'Daniel of his generation, always on the cutting edge of electronics. He was also the first on the street to have a high fidelity record player, then to have true stereo. I remember sitting in his living room, hearing a jet liner land from left to right. What a marvel.

Our first television was a DuMont 19-inch table model. The night we got the new TV, my mother and dad went out for the evening and left my brother and me with a baby sitter. We watched a program on WNCT, Channel 9 called the "Silver Skates." Channel 9 was the first station in our area and was known from "The Capital to the Coast." When word got out to all the teenage girls that we had a new TV, we had little trouble getting sitters.

As a kid, my favorite time to watch TV was after school and on Saturday mornings. The after school programs included Howdy Doody with host Buffalo Bob, Clarabelle the Clown, Princess Summer-Fall-Winter-Spring, Pheneous T. Buster, just to name a few, all cheered on by the studio audience called the "Peanut Gallery."

Another show I particularly liked was called "Pinky Lee." Pinky started each show with his theme song, "Yoo Hoo,

It's me, my name is Pinky Lee....." The best part of the show was that moms would compete against each other in games like putting a pillowcase on a pillow while wearing boxing gloves. The winners always got great kids prizes, like model airplanes and B.B. guns. I wanted, so bad, to bet my mom on that show.

Saturday morning was devoted to either cartoons or half- hour adventures like "The Lone Ranger," "Sky King," and "Rin Tin Tin." Shows like "Roy Rogers" and "Spin and Marty" were left for early prime time.

One particular show that was a huge hit on Saturday mornings was "Winky Dink." It was the first TV show that played on the buying power of the baby boomers. It was also the first interactive TV show in that it required the purchase of a special kit whereby the kids at home could participate in helping the central cartoon character, Winky Dink, to escape from certain perils and defeat the bad guys. The kit included a green piece of Mylar plastic that attached itself to the TV screen. There were also erasable grease pencils so that the kids at home could draw on the screen. One particular peril that I remember was that our hero, Winky Dink was being chased by the bad guy when he came to a canyon. It was up to us to save Mr. Dink, so we were instructed by his human sidekick to draw a bridge across the canyon so that he could get away. As soon as I drew the bridge, Winky crossed to the other side after which I was told to erase the bridge so that the bad guy couldn't catch Winky. One day I decided to ignore the request and not draw the escape route. What I found out was that, Winky really didn't need me. It appeared he'd learned to fly.

Channel 9 remained the only station for a while then one day WITN, Channel 7 appeared out of nowhere. The addition of another network brought an endless amount of programming and by that time, I had moved into prime time, but I'll leave that for another day.

Unlike any other medium, TV has probably done more to change the lives of us all, from the funeral of JFK to the bombing of the Twin Towers. TV has made the world smaller, made us all a part of both triumph and tragedy, yet in many ways brought us together. From a snowy nine-inch screen to the new high resolution, it has made a difference.

Where Have all the Clotheslines Gone?

A few years ago while attending a football game in Greenville, I witnessed a disgruntled fan grab a referee by the neck and slam him to the ground. The next day most of the newspapers led with a caption that read "Referee Clotheslined by Fan." To most of us that lead-in makes sense, but to a future generation, I'm afraid the meaning will soon be lost.

How many of us can remember chasing a little brother or sister across the back yards of our neighborhood, only to be met somewhere between the chest and the neck by one of the many clotheslines that stretched across the yards – meeting the same fate as that ref?

In researching this piece, I drove around town looking for clotheslines and for the most part they are gone. Almost all of the new subdivisions have restrictions against putting one up. But when I was growing up they were as much a part of our lives as the ice cream truck and the mosquito fogger.

Most were simple designs, a pole at each side of the yard, joined by rope or a wire. Some were sturdier than others, made of steel and resembling a telephone pole with two lines. Then some were store bought. Theses devices took up less room and resembled a huge beach umbrella, with a series of lines replacing the fabric. But whatever the design, they were made for one thing, drying clothes. In our neighborhood, there was never a question who wore boxers or briefs. Heck we even knew it they were *Hanes* or *Fruit of the Loom*.

There was also one thing all the clotheslines had in common. Sooner or later they would begin to sag. Rather than to re-stretch the lines, some ingenious soul invented a stick with a bent nail at the end that was used to prop up the clothesline. I've often heard that necessity was the mother of invention, but in our neighborhood I think it was laziness.

And how many times during the summer would a mom gather in the older kids, place the baby back in the crib, and dash out the back door to beat a thunderstorm. Like the buggy whip, clotheslines are quickly disappearing, but for some reason, clean T-shirts don't smell the same and a freshly made bed is not as cool or soft.

Along with the disappearing clothesline, some really great neighborhood services have gone by the wayside. A couple of years ago, the last Pine State milk truck made its rounds through the residential neighborhoods of Raleigh. Here in New Bern, the milkman drove a Maola truck. To the kids of today, it's probably hard to visualize sitting down for breakfast as a man dressed in a white uniform with a black bowtie entered through the back door as he announced, "Milk Man." It is even harder to imagine that he usually knew each member of every household on his route, as he placed milk, ice cream and butter in the kitchen refrigerator.

After a while the milkman stopped coming. I've often wondered if they got together with the doctors and decided to quit stopping by at the same time. Yes, that's right. There was a time when doctors made house calls. It used to be a tradition that when a doctor graduated from medical school, along with his diploma, he got a black leather bag. The bag was something always associated with being a doctor, like a slide rule was for an engineer or an apron for a mason; the bag went with the profession. It also had a function. Like that stick that was designed to hold up the clothesline, the black bag was designed to hold things, things like a stethoscope, a thermometer, tongue depressors, needles, syringes, and of course, penicillin – things the doctor would need when he made house calls. As I remember, the last time a doctor made a professional call to our house, John Baggett came by to see me when I had mono. I think that it was also the last time the milkman paid a visit.

One other guy who used to come around was the garbage man. For years, he walked around to the back of my house and dumped my garbage into his big container. It didn't matter whether I had one or two or even three cans, he'd empty them all. A few years ago, a group of politicians got together and decided that it would be better if we hauled our garbage cans to the street. To add to that humiliating chore, they ruled that we'd have to go out of our way and buy stickers in order to have the cans dumped. It's called curbside pickup.

For some reason it looks like the garbage lobby got to those commissioners, but not in Raleigh. Last week the Raleigh City Council voted down a bill that would have forced curbside pickup on their residents. Although curbside pickup would have saved the city about three million dollars a year, it was the overall opinion of the Council that the continuation of backyard garbage pickup was a "quality of life" issue. I guess in some way that makes up for the traffic.

Recently there has been a division in town regarding the cityscape of New Bern. But rather than look to the sky, maybe we need to look down, not just in the city limits but throughout the county. Just think, if we all joined hands, we could get rid of those unsightly green canisters that stand at attention once a week at our curbside and move backward to a kinder gentler time when "quality of life" did make a difference.

A Changing Landscape

When the Veteran's Administration closed its office in New Bern, my father, with three months severance pay in his pocket, walked the block and a half to the Elk's Building and took the elevator to the second floor to his new office in room 208. His partner, a former mayor by the name of L.C. Lawrence was already at his desk. Together they formed Lawrence and Crayton, a real estate company.

Shortly after World War II ended, those returning vets that Tom Brokaw called the "Greatest Generation" had their eyes on the "American Dream" and the first thing they wanted for their growing families was a new house. Because of that demand, our country saw the largest housing boom in its history. Up north, the migration was from the farms and the cities to the suburbs. Huge construction companies like Levitt and Sons built subdivisions that were so large that many became cities. Today you'll find a Levittown in Pennsylvania, New Jersey and on Long Island.

That boom also filtered down to New Bern. Within months after setting up his business, an old classmate visited my father. Herman Weaver had graduated from Bessemer High School in Greensboro during the depression. My father, Paul Crayton, had been the valedictorian and Weaver had been voted least likely to succeed. The crafty Weaver proved them all wrong.

His purpose for visiting my father was in hopes that dad would help him with a dilemma. His company, Weaver Construction Company, was in the process of building 100 rental houses out by the new high school, currently Grover C. Fields Middle School. His problem was that the houses wouldn't rent.

During his tenure with the VA, my father had helped many a veteran finance a home using the new GI Bill. He showed Weaver the backlog of veterans who wanted to buy houses and convinced him to sell the homes instead of renting them.

My mother set up shop as dad's secretary in a house on Simmons Street, which at the time was a two-lane connector that joined two other two-lane roads – US 17 to the south and US 70 to the west. Dad would pull up to the model/office where a line of cars would be waiting. He'd ask the first one in line to follow him. Once a house had been selected, he'd send the buyer in to the office where my mother took the deposit. My father would then pick the next family in line and start the process all over again. This went on every day for three months. At the end of ninety days, both Herman Weaver and Paul Crayton were smiling. All 100 houses had been sold.

Tryon Village and Trent Park – located just across the right-of-way that would one day lead the four-laned Highway 17 into town – became New Bern's first suburbs. Not as large as a Levittown, they answered a need for the huge number of families riding the beginning of that "Dream." Within no time an elementary school, Trent Park, opened and businesses began to grow around the area. The city limit sign, which stood just west of Chattawka Lane, quickly moved to Simmons Street where it remained until the late '60s. The prison camp on Neuse Boulevard closed and was replaced with what is now one of the premier hospitals in the East.

The houses, modest by today's standards answered a need and, for most of the buyers, was the first home they'd ever owned. Few had garages, the oil furnace stood in the hallway, forcing its hot air around corners. None were air conditioned, let alone insulated. Most were two bedrooms, and the only kitchen appliance offered was a stove. The dishwasher was usually a stay-at-home mom.

While the early '50s saw New Bern's first housing boom it also brought other changes. The Neuse River Bridge that ended at the foot of Johnson Street was torn down to make way for a new one that poured onto Broad Street. That along with the re-routing of Highways 17 and 70 brought on the four-laning of Broad Street which removed the huge oaks that lined the old two-lane street from Five Points to East Front. (Take a mental picture of Pollock Street or National Avenue as it is today and I think you can visualize how Broad Street used to look.)

The old wooden Trent River Bridge, with its gentle curve, was moved from George Street where its approach crossed over the foundation of the main Tryon Palace building, to where it is today at the mouth of the river. The only reminder of that bridge is four poles out in the river that held a sign which said. "Hill's, Known for Good Clothes."

The '50s saw changes but for some reason they took more time to materialize. It was a time for growth, to buy that first house and a time to move up to a two-car family. A time when Eisenhower was accused of being a do-nothing President. I guess we needed those simpler, gentler times, when a Pepsi cost a nickel and kids walked to school, to prepare all of us for what would come next – the turbulent 60's.

Clark's, A Drugstore and a Whole lot More

If you've been by Wal-Mart lately, it seems that they sell just about everything there. About the only thing the one here doesn't sell is cars. Look out Steve Cella, sooner or later they'll probably be selling them as well.

Wal-Mart may be the general store of the new millennium, but they surely didn't invent the idea. Shoot, when I was growing up we had a store here that you might say was the forerunner of the idea Sam Walton has so successfully perfected.

Clark's Drugstore was located on the corner of Middle and Broad in downtown New Bern and it sold just about everything. I guess because it was classified as a drug store, Clark's could dance around the blue laws of the day and stay open on Sunday, just like Wal-Mart. Can you imagine some of the stores today closing on Sunday, of all things?

Since it was located within a block and a half of most of the churchgoers in the town, Clark's soda fountain did a thriving business between Sunday school and church. Sometimes I think as a teenager it was more important to be seen buying your best girl a cherry Coke at Clark's after Sunday School than to actually have been at church.

At Wal-Mart, you can get your haircut, your picture taken, buy drugs and sundries, check out the latest toys, get a hunting or fishing license, even get fitted for a new pair of glasses. Same for Clark's.

Jim O'Daniel, whose MG coupe – in fact, the only MG coupe I've ever seen – stood guard by the back door, while he filled prescriptions and acted as much like a manager as a pharmacist. Chick Natella sold cameras and processed pictures. Other clerks sold guns and ammunition, hunting licenses and toys. And if you needed glasses, you could go upstairs where Dr. Alan Davidson could not only check your eyes, he could check your nose, your ears, and even admit you to Saint Luke's Hospital and take out your tonsils.

Next door, but in the same building, was Service Barber Shop, the largest in New Bern, sporting four chairs. I think they had every issue of *Field and Stream* that had ever been published. At the end of the barbershop Jives Fisher held court, shining shoes – something you can't get at Wal-Mart. Jives was a fixture for as long as I could remember. A man of vast intelligence, he knew every batting record of every baseball player that had ever played the game. Jives popped his rag and made shoes come alive. His finishing touch came from a bottle containing a secret white liquid that when applied to the top of one's shoes made them shine brighter than the hood of one of Don Deichmann's new Cadillacs.

There were two other things you could get at Clark's that are not available from today's Wal-Mart. One was a ride home for a dime. Every hour, four busses pulled into marked spots on the Middle Street side. One went to Ghent, one to Riverside, one went to Duffyfield and one to Bridgeton. Yes, believe it or not, back then we had mass transit and Clark's Drug Store was the downtown depot.

The other thing you could buy at Clark's was a motorcycle. Not just any motorcycle, but one that has become an American legend. A motorcycle whose parent company loves the sound that rumbles from the exhaust pipes so much that they've tried to have that sound trademarked. That's right – the one and only Harley-Davidson.

I guess whoever said that the more things change, the more they stay the same, was not far from the truth. For some reason, whether it's the rumble of a Harley in traffic or the times I put on a pair of freshly shined shoes, or maybe when my throat gets a little sore, a part of me remembers how much Clark's Drugstore, made a difference.

New Bern Golf and Country Club

Right in the middle of Trent Woods there are just over 200 acres of some of the most beautiful property in Craven County. The land belongs to New Bern Golf and Country Club, which has probably had as much influence on New Bern and Trent Woods as has the Trent River.

My first recollection of the club was the long drive leading to the parking lot. Long before Betty Gryb's father, Bob Morrison, planted the majestic live oaks that line the drive so aptly named in his memory, the street was lined with scraggly cedars that ended with a sign that merely stated that "State Maintenance Ends Here."

In the same place where the current clubhouse stands there was a beautiful old building built of cedar shakes with white trim and a green roof. The downstairs of the building housed the locker room, the pro shop and the men's card room. On the main floor there was a ballroom that had a huge fireplace at one end, the ladies card room, and a cocktail lounge. A large room that would eventually become a full-time dining room stretched across the back allowing a beautiful view of the river. Upstairs there was living quarters, generally occupied by an assistant pro or manager. On the front of the building was a full porch, complete with rockers.

There used to be great parties in that old building, especially for the teenagers. The first time I ever heard the Embers, I was fifteen-years-old and double dated with Jim Bryan. That was the first of many fun parties that also included bands like the Blue Notes

Real characters have always been plentiful at the club and some stories cannot be told in a wholesome family newspaper, but members like Bob Pate and B.G. Hines left their mark on the golf course. One story has it that one day Bob Pate birdied the first hole and announced to the other members of his foursome that golf was too easy. He said he wanted a challenge – so he left the green and headed for the card room.

One day Spec Tyson, "Little Billy" Ferebee and Bob Pate were playing on number five, the long par five in the back part of the course, when a small airplane buzzed them and sent them scurrying for cover in the rough. When the airplane did a touch and go on the fairway, they noticed that fellow member B. G. Hines was at the controls. More than likely Benny Baxter was riding in the next seat.

The card room had its share of interesting people as well. Every time I ever went by the card room I saw Shorty Lee and Leland Mason. One day I asked my father if they lived there. He assured me that they did go home from time to time.

The men weren't the only ones who left interesting stories; some women like Thelma Lewis left a legacy. On the right side of the number eight fairway, there are two mounds. Thelma was, shall I say, heavily endowed. One day when she and Katherine Hatley were playing golf, Katherine said the mounds reminded her of Thelma's upper anatomy. . The name "Thelma's Boobs" was born, as the landmarks are still referred to today.

Being a private club, there were several things that one could do at the club that were – let's say – not allowed in other places. For one, the club served liquor by the drink long before the brown bag laws were passed. The other was the presence of two one-armed bandits in the men's card room. One took nickels and the other took quarters. Since the New Bern Police Chief was a member of the club, I knew the slots had to be all right.

There were also many club employees that I remember. There was Leo, and his son Cleo, who tended the greens and fairways as well as the bar in the card room on weekends. There was Levi Bryant who was first the head caddy master, then a greens keeper. Levi was a kind gentle black man from Pollocksville who taught self-esteem to a young white kid from New Bern.

Probably the most controversial employee that I can remember we called "Joe Frog" because of his deep voice and gruff demeanor. Joe presided over the pro shop when Henry Bland was pro, serving up Stewart sandwiches and beer. Kids were not allowed in the pro shop so we ordered from a side window, calling Joe Kent, his real name, "Joe Frog" under our breaths. Joe never did like his nickname, but we sure did.

There have been some great golfers who have belonged to the club but none like the Tyson family dynasty. Spec Tyson won the men's club championship an unprecedented ten times. All of his sons are great players, with Chuck having won the prestigious Men's invitational and Steve recently following his dad's footsteps by winning the club championship.

The Invitational, as it is called was once one of the premiere tournaments in North Carolina. For years Jim and Lib Bryan ran the tournament and produced a great field of players. The short 18-hole course with a par of 70 generally took no prisoners. For many years, some great golfers were never able to win with a sub-par round.

One exciting round took place in the early seventies. After three days there was a four-way tie for the Invitational championship. The tie was between Carl Bell (the local favorite), George Williams, Bob Cato, and Ralph Bogart (Williams and Cato would eventually go on to become multi-winners). On the third hole of the playoff, Cato and Bogart dropped out. Bell and Williams continued for seven more holes. Bell lost on the 10th hole as darkness fell. The gallery had seen a great round of golf.

Before the swimming pool was built the summer activity took place around the beach. Every other year the club hauled in sand and placed it in the roped-off swimming area. The dock was very different then. It was much larger and had a large summerhouse in the middle. At the end of the dock there were two diving boards – one low and one high. The high dive was probably no more than eight feet high, but the view from the top seemed more like fifteen. For the real showoffs, the high dive was not big enough. They could climb on the roof of the summerhouse and dive off the ridge.

The old clubhouse has since been replaced by the current building which sits in the same place as the old one. The new building has been adapted several times and continues to function very well by today's standards. It has charm and elegance. The view of the river is spectacular and the restaurant is one of the best in the area.

The summer activity that took place at the river now centers around the pool, with its new exercise facility. And a few years ago the golf course that challenges the beauty of Augusta National in the springtime, was redesigned and made even more beautiful

The club has grown and now meets the needs of a modern society but every now and then when I pass under the natural canopy that covers Morrison Drive I still get a glimpse in my mind's eye of the glamour that surrounded that grand old building.

Saturday Night Rumble

My cousin Fred and I had just dropped off our dates and headed for the Parkway. It was just after eleven and the August night dripped with humidity. The AM radio tuned to WABC blasted out the newest Four Seasons song. When we pulled up to the drive-in, the parking lot was empty.

"Where is everybody?" Fred asked.

"I almost forgot," I told him. "Drag racing."

"But that's illegal," he said.

"Not at Oak Grove." I answered. "Let's go show 'em what you've got."

My cousin Fred visited me every summer from Washington D.C. This year he brought with him a brand-new 1962 Ford Galaxy 500 XL convertible. His new car had it all. It was red with black bucket seats, had a four-speed transmission and under the hood sported a 390 engine. This machine would fly and we were on our way to Jones County to prove it.

Oak Grove was an abandoned Army Air Corps field located just a few miles west of Pollocksville. At the time, it had not been used since the end of World War II and was easily accessed through a broken-down gate that always stood open. For at least one summer of my life, it held some of the best drag racing I ever saw.

When we pulled through the gate and followed the road that led to the runway, my cousin couldn't believe his eyes. In the middle of one of the most rural counties in North Carolina he saw a collection of some of the most famous muscle cars ever built. "There must over fifty cars," he shouted.

We found a place to park next to a man selling soft drinks from the bed of his pickup. Inside the cab, two small children, dressed in pajamas, slept on the ragged seat. In the middle of the long runway, two of the "grudge racers" approached the starting line. The flagman, a guy from New Bern named Bruce Toler directed the two cars as they inched toward the line. Once in place, Toler pointed his flag at each car. After a ready nod from the drivers, he snapped the flag over his head, followed by revving engines and smoking tires as the two cars roared down the quarter mile course. The brightening of the brake lights told the crowd who'd won.

"Who's the guy to beat?" Fred asked.

"That guy over there," I said.

On the other side of the runway sat a black Chevy Impala Super Sport. Inside, bathed in baby blue light, a man sat in a black bucket seat talking with a girl whose legs stretched all the way to Atlantic Beach. The man's name was Gerald.

"Come on." Fred tugged at his belt as he slowly walked toward the black car.

"He'll eat you alive," I said, following close behind.

"That thing's only got a 327. No way he can touch my 390," Fred boasted.

"It's your car," I said, "but my bet's on the Chevy."

Fred and Gerald, talked for a few seconds, then moments later they lined up next to each other facing Toler with his starting flag. The crowd that gathered on each side of the line swelled to over one hundred – fighting the smell of exhaust fumes mixed with nitro, burnt rubber, and the damp night air.

Toler pointed his flag and both drivers acknowledged that they were ready, their engines revving to a deafening pitch. When the flag snapped, the drivers popped their clutches. With spinning tires, the Ford fishtailed and jumped into the lead, causing part of the crowd to cheer. But Fred's lead would not last long. Gerald went through the four gears so fast, it sounded like an automatic. When he flashed his taillights, the Chevy crowd roared and my cousin limped across in second place.

They don't race at Oak Grove anymore; in fact I was there the night the MPs raided the place. Today the Marines use the base for helicopter training. But for a few years, during the summer months, the sound of squealing tires and open exhausts echoed through the late night air, somehow making a difference to an innocent generation of baby boomers.

Editors Note

Just as the summer of 2004 began, I received a phone call from a man I barely knew. He told me that Gerald Rouse had just passed away. He also told me that Gerald had kept a copy of the article about racing at Oak Grove in the console of his truck. The caller said that Gerald would show it to his friends from time to time. Gerald Rouse was the best drag racer I ever knew and for him to have kept that column is one of the greatest complements this writer has ever had; one that I will always cherish.

I Love Beach Music

I love beach music. I always have and I always will. That's a catchy enough phrase that it would probably make a good song. As a matter of fact it is a song, written by Jackie Gore, the former lead singer of the Embers.

For years, the only exposure to beach music I could get was three hours on Saturdays on Oldies 101 and ten hours on Sundays on WNCT. During the week, however, the music formats on the areas radio stations was limited to oldies, rock, country and classical. It seemed that the Boomers of my generation were being left out.

All that changed last year when Bob Pate, who is the brother of New Bern resident Peggy Austin, put the "Sunny Beach" FM network on the air. By broadcasting from three different stations, all linked together, the network reaches a large audience throughout most of the east. Now I can hear beach music twenty-four, seven.

When most people think of beach music they automatically think of the Pavilion at Atlantic Beach or Sonny's in Cherry Grove or the Pad at Ocean Drive. And, of course, Myrtle Beach. What most people don't know is that New Bern played a huge part in the spread of beach music, which leads me back to the Embers. Unless you have just come from Mars or a Tibetan monastery, you're bound to have heard of the Embers. They are the unofficial ambassadors of beach music. This band has probably done more to spread beach music than all other sources combined. They play an average of six times a week and travel all over the South, proclaiming the sound of rhythm and beach. They play for private parties, concerts, beach music festivals and have even played for an inaugural ball in Washington DC.

Today they travel in a comfortable bus, and their equipment is set up by roadies, just like the name bands. But not long ago things were different. The first time they played in our area was at a dance at the country club. There was Jackie Gore, the lead guitarist and sing, Bobby Tomlinson, the drummer, Durwood Martin who played the keyboards and a saxophone player. They hauled their equipment in a trailer behind Bobby's Grand Prix.

After they played that night at the Club, the Embers were an immediate hit. We could not get enough of these guys. The men at the New Bern Shrine Club wanted to do something for the teenagers in the area, so they booked the Embers for a Saturday night dance the following June.

The Embers dances became so popular that the Shriners booked them for dances twice a month in the summer and once a month in the winter. From the summer of 1962 until the end of summer of 1968, the Embers played at the Shrine Club many times.

Those summer dances drew kids from all over eastern North Carolina. You'd find teenagers from Kinston, Greenville, Jacksonville, Morehead City and Little Washington, as they converged on New Bern to see and dance to the Embers. As the success of the band grew, the cost to continue the dances went up and eventually they were halted. By that time, beach music was following those teenagers who came to town on those hot summer nights to colleges and universities. The music flourished and so did the Embers.

I believe if it had not been for the Shriners, the Embers could have just been another flash in the pan, and beach music would have struggled at best to ever get off the ground. The question always comes up as whether Myrtle Beach or Atlantic Beach is the birthplace of beach music. That question will never be answered, but there is one thing for sure, beach music grew up in New Bern. And one other thing is for sure – the Shriners made a difference.

Mabel, Ring up Mama

A few years ago, after a presentation from a phone company extolling the merits of a new system proposed for the town of Magnolia, the mayor, Mel Pope smiled and addressed the presenter.

Pope, a folksy sort with a sense of humor akin to New Bern Mayor Tom Bayliss, cleared his throat and said, "Sir, I really appreciate the features your new system will provide and I'm sure it will save the town a lot of time and money. But a part of me would rather return to the days when I could pick up the phone and tell Mabel to ring up Mama." After the snickering settled down, he continued, "And she'd say back to me, 'Melvin, I'd be glad to but today is Tuesday and we both know she's over at Bessie's getting her hair fixed.'"

Fast forward to today. Mabel may have been a little more into our business than most of us would like, but at least she was someone we could talk to. How many times when a computerized voice leads us through a menu that ends without the option to speak to a real person, would we love to find a Mabel?

My current phone, for the purpose of local calls has seven digits – my cell phone requires that I dial ten. But the first phone I can remember using only required four. My mom's number was 4832. We also shared the line with one of our neighbors, called a party line. Private lines were for rich people and businesses. With a party line, you could tell when the call was for you by the number of rings. Ours was two. When the phone rang only once, we knew that the call was for the other party. The downside again was privacy. There was a real temptation to eavesdrop, but I'm sure no one ever did that... Right.

Long distance calls were made through an "Operator," a person, usually female, located in a big room down at the Phone Company. To make the call, you'd dial zero and when the operator answered, give her the town, the state and the number you wanted to call. There was no such thing as an area code. If the line was busy, the operator would ask "Sir, the line is busy, would you like for me to keep trying and call you back when I can get through?"

Imagine that. You'd simply hang up, and sometime later the phone would ring and the operator would say something like this. "Sir, I have your party on the line, you can go ahead." That, like the garbage man coming to your back door to pick up the can, is something we'll never see again.

With just four digits to dial, the phone book was about the size of a *TV Guide,* except with fewer pages. But few of us ever used it. We had an unalienable right, run by the Phone Company, called "Information." To access someone's phone number, all we had to do was to dial 1-1-3. A real person, with a pleasant voice would look up the number for us…for free.

As New Bern grew, and the phone system followed, we became more sophisticated. The four-digit number changed to an exchange number – 4832 became Melrose 7-4832. Instead of a numerical area code, each town had its own verbal prefix. I remember that Greensboro numbers were preceded by the word, "Broadway." Before long the name was shortened to the first two letters (ME for New Bern), then to a full seven-digit number. 4832 finally became 637-4832.

Today, everyone has a phone. Many homes have more than one line, serving additional appliances such as fax machines and computers. Even our children carry phones. Our phone books are the size of Sears and Roebuck catalogs and there is a charge for "Information," now called "Directory Assistance."

Since the days of Mabel, where the phone was just a jump or two beyond a couple of tin cans joined by a string, the telephone has evolved into a tool – as much as I hate to say it – none of us can live without. With it we can take and send pictures, send and receive e-mails, and yes, even talk on the confounded thing. We fight with computerized voices and hang up on telemarketers. We slide in and out of voice mails and even know who's on the other end before we answer. But one thing has changed for the better. The telephone is probably the most reliable appliance we've learned to take for granted. I am reminded that recently when Hurricane Isabel came through, spreading devastation throughout the east, most of us experienced power outages – some longer than others. But for the most part, the phones continued to work. That may be worth all the other aggravation put together.

Radio

"Out of the clear blue of the western sky comes Sky King." The first time I heard that sentence was on a Saturday morning, but it did not come from the speaker on our DuMont television set. It came over the airwaves to our Philco radio. I had only to imagine what the "Song Bird," the "Flying Crown Ranch" or even niece "Penny" looked like.

Radio drama, even when it was just for kids, was a lot like reading a book. One's imagination was a part of the experience. Eventually "Sky King" and other shows like the "Lone Ranger" and "Jack Benny" made the transition to television but other popular shows like "The Shadow" with its squeaky door and opening phrase of; "Who knows what evil lurks in the hearts of men? Who knows? The Shadow knows," did not make it.

I even tried my hand at radio drama. One December when I was five, I joined my father along with Colonel A.T. Willis at WHIT radio, which was one of the two stations in New Bern. We were there for a taping of the Charles Dickens classic, "A Christmas Carol," which was to be replayed on Christmas Eve. Colonel Willis played Ebenezer Scrooge, my dad played Bob Cratchet and I played Tiny Tim. My only line, "God bless us, everyone," came at the end of the show.

Eventually radio drama disappeared, only to resurface on the tube. The naysayers predicted radio would die a slow unnatural death. But two things made it possible for radio to continue without losing a beat. Those two things were Rock and Roll and the automobile.

Radio took aim at a younger audience. People like Elvis and Bill Haley echoed from car speakers as teenagers cruised drive-ins on Saturday nights. Programs like "Music 'til

Midnight" serenaded young lovers parked on secluded dirt roads.

We had two stations when radio started its transition. One mentioned earlier was WHIT which held on too long to a dying format. The other, WRNB, was the hip station. It played the new Rock and Roll to the kids who loved it. During the day, WRNB boomed its music throughout the county but as evening fell, the station had to comply with FCC rules and reduce its power. At night WRNB could hardly be heard in Trent Woods, let alone River Bend.

WHIT and WRNB were both AM stations. Radio was divided into AM and FM, because of the signal transmitted. FM stations were known to be clearer, but due to the nature of the signal they had a shorter range than the AM stations. FM was where they played the easy listening music.

In the late 1960s, radio changed again. Two factors influenced that change. One had to do with the automobile again and the other had to do with TV.

Car companies started installing stereo radios. The only signal these radios could receive in stereo was from FM stations. To reach a higher audience, TV stations were raising their transmitting towers by more than a thousand feet, topping many out at two thousand feet. Accompanying a TV antenna at the top of the towers were FM antennas. Now FM stations could reach out hundreds of miles, broadcasting at full signal, 24 hours a day, thereby increasing their market share over the AM stations by more than tenfold. FM, with its better signal, longer range and stereo broadcast brought many AM music stations to their knees.

WHIT and WRNB are not here anymore. Before they left, each tried different formats. Today the big FMs dominate the Rock and Country formats. The AM stations that have survived, usually air talk and easy listening. The good news, however, is that radio did survive.

And now there's XM Radio, and again the car is where the action is. With over 100 channels, many commercial free, this new device, broadcast from satellites – we've come a long way since Sputnik – allows the traveling listener to tune in a station and drive from New Bern to Los Angeles without ever changing a channel or losing the signal. I can't wait to see what's next.

I, for one, am glad that radio didn't die in the 1950s. I think most of us who drive to work each day would agree that no matter what format we listen to, the radio in the dash of our car has made a difference in filling what otherwise would be many a lonely time.

Strawberry

The air raid siren sounded on Wake Island and Strawberry Conderman dashed from his tent, heading for his airplane which was parked just off the hastily completed runway. As he ran toward his aircraft, another pilot had him in his gun sights. When the Japanese pilot squeezed his trigger, the strafing bullets found their mark and brought the young Marine Corps officer to his knees. Conderman died just short of his waiting fighter.

Strawberry Conderman had always been a high achiever. Soon after he lost his mother at age ten, he joined the legendary Troop 13 where he earned the rank of Eagle Scout. After graduating from New Bern High School, he received an appointment to the U.S. Naval Academy where he graduated top of his class. He then took the Marine Corps option and became a naval aviator.

Shortly after Strawberry's death, his father, Fred Conderman received the visit no parent wants to ever experience along with the consolatory letter from the President. Fred Conderman was now alone. His wife and only son had been taken from him. Soon his grief turned to anger and Fred decided that even though he could not replace his son, he was going to do something about it.

In his mid-fifties, Fred tried to join the Marines, the Navy, and then the Army. All the Services turned him down. But Fred was a determined man. His regular job was that of a United States postal inspector. After pulling a few strings, Fred was on his way to the South Pacific. He had been appointed the new postal inspector for Guadalcanal.

When Fred went ashore with the Marines, he bought with him several of his personal rifles that had been bored for military ammunition and had scopes attached. Each morning he would quickly attend to his postal duties then join a Marine patrol. His experience as a hunter and woodsman became obvious. He could spot an enemy sniper before his platoon was in range, then sneak up on the sniper and take him out. Needless to say, Fred Conderman was popular with the Marines and very much in demand. The Marine commander on Guadalcanal was quoted as saying that many a young American owed his life to Fred Conderman.

I knew Mr. Conderman, not from this story, which I learned about many years later, but for what he did for children who grew up in New Bern. Fred lived on the Trent River. His house was on a large piece of land where Lieutenant Governor Perdue now lives. When he returned home, Fred turned his front yard into a playground for kids. There was a dock with a diving board, a rope swing in a tree where you could swing out over the river and drop in the water, and a long cable with a pulley attached. We'd climb to a platform built on one of the cypresses in Fred's yard, grab the pulley then zoom along the cable until we reached speeds of up to a bazillion miles and hour, only, to let go and splash into the Trent River.

I never knew Strawberry Conderman. My generation's war in Southeast Asia started some thirty years after his death. But he and I share two things, an Eagle badge from Troop 13 and a great respect for his father. Fred Conderman risked his life to avenge the death of his son then returned home to celebrate his life by making a place for kids who never knew Strawberry, to have some fun. To that man who sat quietly on his screened porch while a bunch of neighborhood kids swam, and swung and dived, thank you. Fred Conderman, you made a difference.

The Lessons of Floyd

Alan Hoffman and Elizabeth Wilder don't live in New Bern, but from time to time they come into our living rooms, so to most of us they seem as familiar as our next-door neighbors. For seven days and nights in late September the team from Channel Nine lived with us, covering Hurricane Floyd and the flooding that followed. Along with co-anchors Jeff Rivenbark and Stephanie Cornwell and meteorologists Phillip Williams, Ben Smith and David Sawyer, they kept us informed of Floyd's fury, through words and pictures.

But most importantly, I think, is that they stayed with eastern North Carolina until the flood waters began to subside. Even sportscaster Bryan Bailey got into the act, helping to load the more than ten and a half tractor-trailers that were sent out to bring aid to the victims. And if that was not enough, WNCT also raised over one hundred thousand dollars for the relief effort.

We are very fortunate, those of us who live in New Bern. Normally when a hurricane hits, we are the ones who suffer the wrath of the storm. But this time our brothers to the West and North have felt the aftermath of what will probably be the most devastating storm to ever hit our state.

Shortly after Floyd passed, many heroes became airborne in efforts to save those stranded people captured by rising waters. The air space over Edgecombe County was so crowded that an airborne control center was launched. These brave members of the Army, The Coast Guard, and the Marine Corps need to be commended for doing their jobs.

While most took to the air to save lives, some became airborne looking for someone to blame, trying to find someone to point a finger at what some call an act of God. Floyd was not an act of God, it was an act of nature. The love given by the people of our state to their brothers and sisters in eastern North Carolina was and continues to be what I call an act of God.

To many all seemed lost. Then on a magical night in Raleigh, everything stopped for four hours. On a borrowed field, a torn and tattered football team from East Carolina took on another "Hurricane." That night the Pirates were supposed to lose, but their victory over the University of Miami taught us to never give up.

I believe the team from Channel 9, the many rescuers, the public safety people, the ECU football team, and each and every one of you who read this and have helped and continue to help with the recovery have indeed made a difference.

Walt Bellamy

One thing you don't see any more is a hitchhiker. Maybe it's because today, almost everyone has a car or maybe because hitchhikers are considered dangerous. Whatever the reason, you just don't see them any more.

That certainly wasn't the case when I was growing up. From the time a boy turned fourteen, when it was no longer cool to still ride a bike, until he was old enough to drive, it was the preferred means of transportation.

Heck, I can remember many a Sunday afternoon during my freshman year at Carolina, when it was forbidden by the school to have a car on campus; my dad would take me to the corner of Race Track Road and Highway 70 and let me out. I would produce a shirt cardboard on which I'd scrawled the letters UNC, hold it up to oncoming traffic, and four rides and two to three hours later, I'd wind up back in Chapel Hill.

Probably the most traveled road for hitchhikers in our area was Country Club Road, which linked the clubs in Trent Woods to the neighborhoods of New Bern. Today as I travel that same road between work and home, I never see a single hitchhiker, but back in the early '60s, especially on the weekends, we were all over the place.

I bummed so many rides on that road that most have faded from my memory. But one is still as fresh in my mind as it was in 1961.

One day, on our way back into town, Dale Goldman and I stuck out our thumbs and shortly a green 1955 Ford four-door sedan stopped to give us a ride. Driving the car was a kindly black man who introduced himself as Mr. Bellamy. On the way into town, he asked us if we followed sports, especially, basketball. When I told him that I was the manager of the New

Bern High School team, he asked me if I'd ever heard of Walt Bellamy.

When I told him no, the kindly Mr. Bellamy said that Walt was his son, that he was from New Bern and that he played for Indiana. But that's not what really impressed me.

As we arrived at our destination, Mr. Bellamy pulled over to let Dale and me off. Before we got out, he reached in a bag that sat next to him on the front seat and produced a large gold medallion. He let us examine it closely. Now, I was impressed. What I held in my hand was an Olympic Gold Medal, the one his son had won for basketball in the 1960 Rome Olympics.

That day a beaming father told his son's story, showed us newspaper clippings, and shared his pride, all to a couple of young white kids he'd never met. From that day forward I've felt the same pride for a man I've never met. Whenever his name comes up I always say, "We're from the same town."

Walt Bellamy went on to play in the NBA for 14 years and in 1993 he was inducted into the NBA Hall of Fame. Oh yes, and the next time you turn right off of Country Club Road onto Walt Bellamy Drive, remember this, that street is named for one of the greatest basketball players who ever lived. I'll never forget the ride Mr. Bellamy gave me that day and the difference he made in my life.

Ralph Miner. A Golf Pro with a Heart of Gold

Before we moved to Trent Woods, I lived on Lucerne Way in town. Trent Woods wasn't even Trent Woods back then, it was called Country Club Heights, probably because of New Bern Golf and Country Club.

I remember as a youngster, back in the late '50s and early '60s, that the club was way out of town. We'd pack a bunch of kids into the back of Pat Jones' 1958 Olds station wagon, and we'd take the long ride down Country Club Road to go for a swim at the club. That was before they built the pool. My mom and Pat would bring lunch along and we'd spend the day at the river.

Country Club Road was not much different back then except that there were only a handful of houses and the speed limit was fifty-five. I can still see Pat driving that huge brown and white car, her arm out the window, roaring along that winding road. It seemed as if it took forever to get to the club from town.

Today much has changed. New Bern Golf and Country is not in the country anymore, but surrounded by New Bern and Trent Woods. No one goes for a swim in the river, opting for the pool, and anyone driving down Country Club Road over thirty-five miles an hour had better plan on getting a ticket.

One thing has not changed. Several years ago my father took me to the Masters in Augusta, Georgia. I was amazed at how much that famous championship course had in common with the one in New Bern. It probably had a lot to do with the time of year. In about ten days, the golf course in New Bern will rival any in the south. Spring does its magic and, like Augusta National, New Bern will be ablaze with color. The dogwoods and azaleas will paint a scene worthy of a Monet watercolor.

For those of us fortunate to drive by the club this time of year and to enjoy its beauty, we owe a great deal to a man by the name of Ralph Miner. Miner was the son of McDearment Miner, who has been recognized by the USGA as the first American born golf professional. All the other professionals before Mr. Miner came from Scotland.

Mr. Miner had four sons. All of them became golf professionals and, as was expected, were extremely good tournament players. Word has it that when the Miner boys played in a tournament, they wore kilts to celebrate their Scottish heritage. What's left of Ralph Miner's kilt is on display in the clubhouse.

Ralph Miner followed the circuit by playing golf up north in the summer and coming south for the winter. One day he stumbled on the little nine-hole fledgling course at New Bern. Ralph liked it so much, and the members liked him so much, that he agreed to stay and be the first golf professional at New Bern.

When the stock market fell, the club also fell on hard times. In 1935, New Bern Savings and Loan foreclosed on the club and it was sold at the courthouse door. Afraid that the club would cease to exist, Ralph Miner, the paid professional who ran the club, bought it for just over five thousand dollars.

For the next few years, Miner ran the club for the members, just as he'd done before. He'd always promised to sell it back to them. In 1943, Miner sold the club back to the members. True to his form, he kept his word and sold it back for exactly what he'd paid for it. A few years later, Ralph Miner retired and went back up north. When he died in 1949, the Miner family honored his wishes and he was buried in New Bern Cemetery, just off Chelsea Road, less than half a mile from his beloved country club.

As I am writing this, I am looking out my window at the remarkable beauty that spring brings to that little golf course. Had it not been for that man of honor, I truly believe that that beauty would not exist today. Who knows, maybe there would be no golf course and maybe not even a Trent Woods. Ralph Miner made a difference.

September 11, 2001 – A Day That Brought Us All Back Together

My heart is heavy as I write this month's column. Last week a dastardly group of cowards attacked the United States. By the time you read this, I'm sure the fatalities in the twin towers could be more than five thousand, and those in Washington will be in the hundreds.

The attacks on both the World Trade Center and the Pentagon, were not just attacks on our country, they were attacks on each and every one of us. I have taken what those criminals did personally. Last week it seemed more like someone in my family had died. I found myself fighting back tears at the oddest moments. Now I'm mad.

When the Japanese attacked Pearl Harbor that fateful day in 1941, General Yamamoto made the statement that he'd awakened a sleeping giant. Last Tuesday, whether he likes it or not, Osama bin Laden and his group of cutthroats, startled that giant awake again. He and those who support his hatred of us, have no idea what we are like when we're riled.

For the most part, we are a peaceful society, wanting to live and let live. But when someone hurts one of us, he hurts us all. As President Bush put it, for those who did this heinous act; we will hunt you down and find you. Make no mistake in the resolve of the American people.

Other cultures don't understand us. Ours is a free society, and a free society is an open society. Oft times we air our dirty laundry in public. Those that see the bickering we do between ourselves think it to be discord and distrust. They see differences between Northerners and Southerners, blacks and whites, Democrats and Republicans and view those differences as chinks in our armor. But like a big family that occasionally fights among themselves, that family will also stand together when threatened. When we come out of the chute, we come as a raging bull.

Adolph Hitler called us a mongrel race. The smartest and strongest dog I ever had never had papers. That mongrel race he looked down on almost single-handedly sent Hitler to his bunker where he took his own life.

When I was growing up, the Empire State building was the tallest building in New York. New York was the gateway to America. Those who first came to our shores saw the Statue of Liberty as a symbol of freedom and the Empire State building as a symbol of our power and strength. Today, that same building again stands alone as the tallest building in New York. Let its red, white, and blue spire remind us that we are still the greatest nation in the world.

We are as diverse a people as any on the planet. We come from all walks of life and every ethnic background. But there is one thing that transcends all others and that is the fact that we are Americans first.

In recent years it has become politically correct to preface our Americanism with an ethnic title. We call ourselves Latin-Americans, Cuban-Americans, Afro-Americans, Anglo-Americans, Irish-Americans, German-Americans, Native-Americans, and many others. We are all proud of our heritage and ancestry, as we should be, but today I'm suggesting that we drop the prefixes and let the world know that we are all one nationality, Americans.

Unlike the war of my generation, we are united. We can now show the world what it is like to stand together and defeat a common enemy. We have the opportunity to join the generation of our parents and become the "Greatest Generation" of the Twenty First Century. Together, we WILL make a difference.

Bands

The first high school dance I can remember attending was just before school started my freshman year. It was a street dance held in a downtown parking lot just off Broad Street. I couldn't wait to get there and hear the live music we were promised. The NBHS dance band was playing that night.

Visions of Bill Haley and his Comets danced in my head only to be replaced in reality by something closer to Glenn Miller. Boy, was I disappointed. That's right. They were playing our parents' music, not ours. And none of us knew how to foxtrot.

Our music – Elvis, The Platters, The Drifters – was all over the radio, on records sold at Hawk's and filling the racks of most juke boxes, but to hear it live we had to go to places like Faison or The Pavilion at Atlantic Beach. It seemed that the only music the dance band knew was Cole Porter and George Gershwin.

By the time my junior year rolled around, all that changed. The Embers, the most successful beach band of all times, were being booked five or six times a year at the Shrine Club. It was not long before the NBHS dance band slowly disappeared. "Night and Day" was being replaced by "Night Train." The old music of our parents' generation was finally on its way out – we thought.

When my class left for college, bands like the Embers began to migrate to the Triangle area for the winter where their fan base was now located. A huge void for live rock and roll was left. It was soon filled, not by groups from some far away place like Raleigh, but right under the bear's nose.

David Erdman loved his guitar. After the folk era ended, most of us "would be pickers" set down our acoustic six strings, never to be picked up again. But not David, he went electric. To fill the empty space left by the dance band and the beach bands that were not frequenting the area, he formed a group called The Summits. The band was comprised of teenagers from the halls of New Bern High, most of them not old enough to drive. Mike Zaytoun, the drummer, told me that after Erdman left for Duke, he had the band booked on college campuses for fraternity parties. Mike said that he and the other members of the band would borrow a car from one of the parents, hook up the trailer with all the instruments and Mike would drive to Durham or Chapel Hill, since he had the only driver's license. I wonder how many parents would let that happen today.

Along with David Erdman, Jay Smith played lead guitar. The other members of the band were Jay Jones and Barry Langston on bass, Alex Holton and Jessie Nelson on trumpet, Ken Powell on keyboards and Tom Ward, lead singer.

Not to be outdone by his older brother, Ted Erdman who chose the bass over the guitar, formed The Impacts. His group included Tim Coates as the lead guitarist along with David McFayden on drums, Charles Meekins on trumpet, and John Thomas on keyboards. Like The Summits that preceded them, The Impacts chose soul music and rhythm and blues over The Beatles.

Both bands were very active around New Bern playing for sock hops and dances at the Episcopal Parish House. While The Summits enjoyed the college party circuit, The Impacts played closer to home, opting for NCO and Officer Clubs aboard the nearby military bases.

Tim Coates said that after every gig, most of the guys would finish out the evening at Tony's, an all-night drive-in located in Bridgeton. One night at the ripe old age of sixteen, he and John Thomas, after downing a couple of burgers, started home. When they hit the intersection of First and Pollock, they were sideswiped by another car. The car, which failed to stop, took out their taillight. The next day, they popped another one in and kept on trucking.

In a time when school systems are trying to cut subjects like art and music education and some parents think that joining a band is a waste of time, it might be a good idea to let some of those people know what became of those musicians that formed

The Summits and The Impacts. Unfortunately Ted Erdman died at an early age in a car accident but the rest haven't fared so badly. David Erdman is a lawyer in Charlotte and has served on the Charlotte City Council. Jay Smith, an insurance executive in Florida, has a vote in the Grammy Awards. Tom Ward is a successful New Bern lawyer. Mike Zaytoun, along with his brother Jackie, owns one of the largest cabinet manufacturing companies in the east. Jay Jones, who would later go on to play with Gene Barber and The Cavaliers, is a computer executive in Virginia Beach and Barry Langston teaches music in the Carteret Country School System. As for Alex Holton, he has a Ph.D. in music education and when he is not playing with the Metropolitan Opera in New York, is the first trumpet for the Long Island Philharmonic. Still here in New Bern are Tim Coates who is the owner of New Bern Auto Supply and the NAPA store; John Thomas owns a successful engineering firm; Charles Meekins is a retired Navy captain and well known stockbroker, and David McFayden is our very own District Attorney.

On Oct. 17th and 18th, my high school class – the class of 1964 – is holding its 39th reunion. On Saturday night we're planning a dinner dance with the music being provided by Middle Street Moods. I'm sure they'll play a little beach music, but most of what we'll hear are songs we now call "standards;" you know – Cole Porter and George Gershwin. For some reason, we've fallen in love with our parents' music and that night when Tommy Hall sings a Sinatra ballad backed up by two old members of the NBHS dance band, Winston Dixon and Robert Tyson, maybe we'll realize how much of a full circle we've made.

A Wartime Christmas

Officially, we have only been at war twice during the last one hundred and one years, but we all know that many times semantics and political correctness share the same bed.

In fact we have been at war five times. If you count Bosnia, Somalia, Grenada, and Panama, the count goes up to nine. But until now, it has been over ten years since our troops have been in a truly hostile environment during the Christmas season.

One day my cousin, Fred, and I were sitting on the beach sharing the newspaper. He finished reading an article about some famous person who had, after a bout with depression, taken his own life. Fred put the paper in his lap and looked at me.

"No American in his right mind should ever think about taking his life, let alone be depressed." He continued to say that all of us need to be thankful. Thankful that we live in this great country.

Fred reminded me that day that even the homeless in the United States have it better than some of the wealthiest people in other places in the world. Just being born an American was a privilege and a gift from God – something we all needed to be thankful for.

As I said in one of my previous columns, Thanksgiving is one of my favorite days of the year. Over the years, I've been concerned that the Christmas season would overshadow that day, unique only to the United States and Canada. Recently, I've had somewhat of a change of heart. I still feel that Thanksgiving is a most special day in that it allows us time to thank our Creator for the many blessings He's given us. But I now see Thanksgiving as much more. It kicks off a season of joy and giving that is finally highlighted by a day dedicated to the birth of Christ. I now see that the two days go together, hand in hand.

My wife, Jane, used to say she wished the Christmas season was more like the ones depicted in Courier and Ives prints. She's often said that she'd like to see each person give only one present – one that he or she had made – to those loved ones on their list. I've told her to do so would probably bring the US economy to its knees. I think that maybe there is a way to show the meaning of Christmas and still support our economy.

This season, when you feel stressed and short on time, stop for a moment and think of the men and women who are giving of themselves, in harms way, so that we can be free. Think of their families who'll be spending this Christmas without them. Take time while searching through the stacks of merchandise, looking for that object your loved one wants that is impossible to find and smile at the person next to you. Don't wait for Christmas Eve to wish that stranger in the parking lot a "Merry Christmas." Do something that will make a difference in someone else's life and don't forget to thank God that you are an American.

Cops

I seem to sleep better lately, at least better than I did twenty years ago. It's not so much that I go to bed earlier, although that surely plays a part in it, but a great deal of that rest comes from knowing that the Trent Woods police are somewhere out there.

The first police officer that I can remember was Joe Grey. He had been on the Havelock force and became our first and only cop. His main job was to bring speeding in Trent Woods to a halt, which he did, as many of our residents can attest to.

Before Joe, most of the town was on its own. There wasn't even a regular sheriff's deputy assigned to the town and vandalism, speeding and even an occasional break-in took place.

Twenty years ago, Trent Woods wasn't as large as it is now. Much of Country Club Hills and all of Fox Hollow lay in a no-man's land between New Bern and Trent Woods. At that time I lived on Canterbury Road and it appeared that neither New Bern nor Trent Woods wanted us.

While Joe was busy cleaning up the speeders and the break-ins, those of us in places like Canterbury Road had to resort to hiring a private cop to patrol our area at night. His name was Marion White and he went on duty at dusk and patrolled his areas until morning, using a mobile phone for communication.

There were several times that I remember calling Marion to ride by and make sure that that bump in the night that my wife had heard was just that and not a potential robber.

One particular night, even I heard the noise. The bang that came from downstairs continued even as I called out from the stair landing and threatened to call Marion.

Finally I made the call. After I hung up, I called Ken McCotter, who lived behind me, for back-up. As soon as Marion arrived I met him at the front door. We immediately searched the downstairs for an intruder, but none was to be found. As soon as our search was abandoned, I called to Ken and gave him the all clear. Ken appeared from behind a tree in his pajamas, carrying his shotgun. Atop his head was his hunting cap.

For a few minutes, the three of us chatted, only to be startled by the clanging sound I'd heard earlier. All three of us froze, guns drawn. Before anyone moved, the noise got louder, then my old bird dog Beau appeared at the crawl space doorway and came outside. It seemed that old Beau had fallen asleep between some galvanized heating ducts and when he stood to shake off the sleep, he'd bumped into them, sending the racket through the house.

About that same time there had been a huge fire at the Yacht Club. All of the docks had been lost along with many boats. The Yacht Club decided, in order to protect the property and boats, to hire a night watchman. He worked there for several years.

With the advent of the new Trent Woods policeman, the hired cop, and the night watchman, the local teenagers of the time, namely Hovey Aiken, Billy Rawls, Hubie Tolson and "Super Dave" Kunkel, decided to give them nicknames. They were called "Trent-a-pig," "Rent-a-pig," and "Pajama-pig," respectively.

Today the Trent Woods police department is one of the most respected in the area. Chief Tony Smith and officers Mike Register, Charles Strunk, and Barry Johnson, have made our town one of the most peaceful in North Carolina. Break-ins are almost a thing of the past. Tony and his men keep an eye on the community. To paraphrase a Beach Boys' song, "The bad boys know 'em and they leave 'em alone."

Tony says that the worst things they have to deal with now are vandals but that was not the case a few years ago when a major crime was committed in our town. Although the local sheriff's department as well as the SBI had been called in, it was the Trent Woods police who solved the crime.

Yes, I think we can all sleep better because of the Trent Woods police. Chief Smith, I think I speak for all the residents of Trent Woods when I say that you and your officers make a difference.

JFK – Our President

When a national tragedy occurs, we can all remember exactly where we were and what we were doing. To the current generation it will probably always be September 11, 2001. For Generation X it will more than likely be when the space shuttle exploded and for my parent's generation, it will surely be December 7, 1941 when the Japanese attacked Pearl Harbor. But for my generation it has to be November 22, 1963, the day John Kennedy was killed.

For me it's hard to believe that on Saturday, 40 years will have passed since the Kennedy assassination. In some ways it seems like yesterday when a choked-up Walter Cronkite slipped his glasses off, turned his head toward the clock in his studio and told a horrified America that the President had died, some thirty-eight minutes earlier.

The events of that weekend are chronicled on film and video tape, but for most of us, it is burned in our memories – the riderless horse with the boots turned backward, Jackie kissing the casket as her husband's body laid in state under the Capital rotunda, the drone of the muffled drums, the long line of mourners, and of course, 4-year-old John-John saluting as the caisson carrying his dad passed by. No matter what our politics are today, at the time – to most baby boomers – the dashing young JFK was our President and for him to die from an assassin's bullet was beyond belief.

Names like Oswald, Ruby, Conley and Johnson have become so familiar that many can be used as metaphors. And will the controversy ever end? Was Lee Harvey Oswald the only shooter? Was the President's death a Cuban, Russian, Mafia, or even a political conspiracy? Was there a cover up? There are as many theories as questions but, only one unclear answer.

In his short time as President, Kennedy was confronted with more crises than most Presidents incur in two full terms. Some he handled brilliantly, like the Cuban Missile Crisis, which history has proven avoided nuclear war. Others, like the Bay of Pigs fiasco, he botched. And there were some, like the construction of the Berlin Wall, he could do little about.

Kennedy's choices of high-level aides and advisors were as varied as his accomplishments. His closest circle of advisors was headed by his brother Bobby and access to that circle was very limited. David Halberstam, in his book "The Best and the Brightest," unfolds how JFK surrounded himself with the smartest and most politically astute men in the country. For the most part he was right. People like Dean Rusk at State and our own Luther Hodges at Commerce were among his cabinet members. Also, none of us will ever forget Adlai Stevenson's verbal attack on the Russian ambassador to the UN during the missile crisis.

But there were others that history would define as poor choices, most formidably, Secretary of Defense Robert McNamara. He would follow Lyndon Johnson into the next administration and McNamara's hands would forever be stained by the deaths of thousands of American solders in a war he allowed to continue.

Kennedy was kind of a bridge between the tranquil '50s and the turbulent '60s. Mirrored by events of his presidency, the coming years would bring more change than most of the preceding decades, especially social change.

The mismanagement of war in Vietnam escalated and split the nation, resulting in violent clashes among the citizens. Hippies burned their draft cards and those of us with a since of duty returned home to an apathetic greeting, at best. The final stab in the heart came when National Guard troops fired on their own people at Kent State.

Along with the division caused by the war, the Civil Rights movement headed by Martin Luther King brought on more unrest. Peaceful marches and sit-ins ended many times with fire hoses, police dogs and in some cases, death. Like the President, his brother Bobby and Dr. King were both assassinated.

But in 1969 as the decade drew toward its end, the nation stopped and held hands as we watched on our very own TV sets, one of Kennedy's dreams come true. Neil Armstrong stepped from the ladder of the LEM onto the surface of the moon, making a giant leap for mankind.

From the hope of the 1960 election until the Apollo landing, America had changed in other ways.   Things like fallout shelters, color TV, "Laugh-In," muscle cars, mini-skirts, Dr. Zhivago, tie-dye, beach music, Mo-Town, Bonnie and Clyde, the Beatles, bra burning, long hair, shag carpet, harvest gold appliances, bell-bottom pants, and polyester suits made their way onto the scene. Some quickly disappeared and others made their impact on our future. But one thing came out of the '60s and made a difference; it was the decade that made us think. It was a decade started by the election of a dynamic young President whose short time in the White House left a mark that would carry on for years to come.

The Summers seemed cooler and the Winters warmer

I didn't always live in Trent Woods. I spent my early years at 1800 Lucerne Way, the last house on a street that gently sweeps into Tryon Road.

As hot as August seems to me today, for some reason those days growing up in middle class America with no air conditioning didn't seem so hot and one TV channel appeared just about right. The daytime sky was always a deep blue with white puffy clouds and the nights were cool. Summer vacation was the best time of the year.

Our neighborhood was full of kids. It seemed there were at least three to each household. I guess that's why today we're called boomers. The first person my age that I remember meeting when we moved to our new house was Paul Johnson. He had a chain driven tricycle that could maneuver on the two dirt streets we all lived on and his mom allowed him to go around the block. That friendship, along with ones with Dale Goldman and Mike and Jimmy Jones, have lasted a lifetime.

Summer days were filled with fun. We'd take a nickel from our twenty-five cent allowance and go to Mrs. Flower's store where most of my friends would buy a Coke. I'd buy a Pepsi, not because it was a native product, but because it had four more ounces. Of course when the drinks were finished, I didn't get the chance to "Travel" with the Coke drinkers. On special days, if I had another nickel, I'd buy a bag of peanuts and pour them straight into the bottle and drink it, peanuts and all.

There were also a lot more soft drinks to choose from. We had Blue Pat, Nehi, Orange Crush, Dr. Pepper, R.C, 7-Up,

TruAde, and as my brother used to say to the store attendant, "Mister, do you have some of those 'delisus' 'socklit' drinks?" I was really disappointed when they raised the price to six cents. No more five to a quarter.

It wasn't long before they brought the treats to us. The Dairy Queen truck, with its tinkling bell would show up close to three in the afternoon, followed by the snow cone truck. Grape was my favorite flavor.

Each summer we always put on a circus at the Jones' house. Leslie Morris would be the ringmaster and I was always the strong man. Our menagerie was filled mostly with our dogs, dressed up in outfits to resemble wild lions and tigers. Jimmy Jones was always the star. After the parade and clown skits, he'd come to center stage and perform on the trapeze that hung on the swing set. All the kids in the neighborhood would either participate or come to the show. We even charged admission and sold soft drinks. One thing has always bothered me. I never knew what happened to the money. For some reason I suspect that's how the Jones family started Carolina Dry Kiln.

In those days, most of our mothers stayed home, tending to the kids and the household. I can still picture my mother, a baby on her hip, hanging clothes on the clothesline in our backyard; visiting with our neighbors across the small wire fence that separated our yards. Supper, as we called it, was usually on the table by the time our fathers got home and washed up. And after it was over, we'd dash outside and play with the other neighborhood kids until dark.

As I grew older, my parents let me go to Fort Totten for the church league baseball games. At fourteen-years-old, that was the place to be seen, not so much for the games, but that's where the girls were. The summer before my best friend Shelly Steinberg died, we had the times of our life at that park. We'd meet at the corner of Tryon Road and First Street and make our way through DeGrafenreid Park, stopping under one of the huge oaks that lined the way, to steal a smoke in the August twilight. Once at the park, we'd meet up with our other friends and do what teenagers trying to act grown up did; mostly say stupid things to the girls who tried to look as if they were ignoring us.

I guess that year was the one where those simple summers changed for me. That fall I entered the freshman class at New Bern High. Before Thanksgiving, Shelly had been killed in a car crash. It was the first time I had lost a friend and he was my best friend. I think it was the first time I became aware of my own mortality.

From then on for me, summer days were spent at other places; house parties at the beach, skiing on the river, or just hanging around the Trent Pines Club. And summer nights were not whiled away at Fort Totten anymore, my friends and I graduated to meeting all the other high school chums at the Parkway drive-in.

For some reason the kids today seem to be bored and to interact more with machines than with each other. A lot of them want to spend summers inside. I guess the lack of air conditioning gave us the opportunity to interact with each other and for that I am thankful. Those days on Lucerne Way will forever be etched in my memory as a time when simple things like playing neighborhood games on someone's front yard on a still August night or watching a little league ball game allowed us to be kids.

Middle Street

Two old men sat on a bench next to a water fountain that had been fashioned from a ship's cannon. They seemed more interested in the checkerboard that sat between them than the old red truck as it pulled up to the intersection of Middle and Pollock Streets. When the truck came to a stop, a pair of city workers got out and struggled with a four-sided sign in the bed. Once the sign had been firmly placed in the metal pipe countersunk in the center of the intersection, one of the men looked at the clock tower that hovered above city hall. "Five minutes early," he told his partner as they climbed back into the truck and drove away. Only minutes later did the clock strike nine times and the four-sided sign announced to all that for this Saturday, as with all Saturdays, that the intersection was a "No Turn" zone. Kinston boasted its "Magic Mile," but we had Middle Street.

In the days when I grew up in New Bern, Middle Street was the center of all activity. The mall had not come yet and Sam Walton seemed to be happy with his Arkansas department store. It was a time when the downtown teemed with people, especially on Saturdays. Dragging Middle was a must. To a bunch of young high school boys with new drivers' licenses, it was a place to be seen and check out the girls. For some reason it felt like someone was bringing them in by the busload.

Shopping was what it was all about. The big stores were all there: Belk's, Penney's, Montgomery Ward, and Sears. Then there were the mid-sized ones: Charles Store, Copeland-Smith, and Lipman's, as well as the two dime stores (imagine buying something for a dime) S.H. Kress and McLellan's. Those stores were followed up by specialty shops such as Hill's (where they sold Weejuns and Gant shirts), The Smart Shop, The Fashion

Center, The Parisian, The Bootery, Merritt Shoes, Fagan Electric, Hawk's Radio (where the white RCA dog stood guard by the front door),Turner-Tolson Furniture, The Hobby Shop, and Baxter's Sporting Goods (the only source in town for Johnson Outboards and Converse All-Star tennis shoes). Today, only three of the businesses have outlasted the rest and are still going strong: Benners Studio, Bynum's Drugstore, and Mike's Jewelers.

There were also some good places to eat. Remember the cream-filled donuts at Craven Bakery or the pizzas at Louis's. And who could forget the grilled chicken salad sandwich served at Gaskin's Soda Shop. How about a Greek salad at Williams Restaurant – known from Maine to Florida – or dining over the water at Nelson's, as Middle Street became a tributary of the Trent River? And of course the dime stores both had lunch counters. One year we went to Kress (we called it Kressie's) for my mother's birthday. They were having a special – first breakfast for forty-nine cents. The rest of the family ate for a penny a person.

My last two years in high school, I had a Saturday job working at Belk's in the shoe department. I loved that job, especially helping out girls my own age. I think everybody in New Bern knew the white haired Mr. Flowers who ran the department.

One device that I remember all respectable shoe stores had was something called a "shoe fitting x-ray machine." Basically it was a fluoroscope. The customer tried on the shoes, then placed his or her feet under the machine. The resulting image of the feet within the shoes could be viewed through three ports – one for the customer, one for the salesman, and another for a third person (maybe a parent). Just think, a whole generation nuked its feet twice a year while mom or dad looked on.

Today Middle Street has changed. You can turn left or right at the Middle-Pollock intersection, even on Saturdays. But we are fortunate. When the stores started leaving or going out of business, we did not follow suit with Raleigh and Greenville and "Mall Off" our main street. Better wisdom came forth from our downtown business and property owners. Swiss Bear was formed and a special tax district created. Now our downtown rivals any in the state. Some call us a reflection of Annapolis. I say better. We don't have the traffic. Trees grow from our brick paved sidewalks and shops, bars and cafes draw clientele to a section of town that is fun as well as safe both day and night. And what we have today is just a bud on the flower. The full blossom is on its way. Middle Street, there's something about you I really like. Keep on making a difference.

Mother's Day

Mothers Day came and went last weekend as it does every year. For me, it has always been the unofficial beginning of summer, a time to start thinking about going to the beach. For some reason, however, this year Mother's Day took on a different meaning – actually the real reason that we recognize the holiday. It is a celebration of our mothers.

Celebrations honoring mothers can be traced back to ancient Greece where the Greeks paid tribute to Rhea, the Mother of the Gods. In England, they honored mothers on "Mothering Sunday" which was celebrated in the 17th century on the fourth Sunday of Lent.

Celebration of Mother's Day in the United States began in 1910 in West Virginia and by 1911 nearly every other state had set aside a day for mothers. In 1914, President Woodrow Wilson, through a Presidential proclamation, made the second Sunday in May the official day of the new national holiday, Mother's Day

The credit for Mother's Day is not clear. Some historians say that the holiday was inspired by Anna Jarvis to honor her mother. Others give credit to Frank E. Hering of South Bend, Indiana, honoring the mothers of dead soldiers. No matter who was the driving force behind Mother's Day, today the holiday is celebrated throughout the world.

Today, at least for me, Mother's Day is a special day. It reminds me of those special things only a Mom can do. I think of the time she sat up all night with me when I had a fever. I remember that without her help with Nature Merit Badge I'd never have gotten my Eagle Scout award, and how proud she was of me. I remember the time when my best friend died that she helped me come to grips with his passing and work through the pain of losing him.

Mothers are the most special of special people. They have a way of kissing things and making them better. I'm sure that those who read this article will remember those times when only their mom could make things better, when a smile or a loving hug was all that was needed. If you're lucky enough to still have your mother and didn't call her last Sunday, why not do it now. I'm sure in your life she.....made a difference.

Two Great Teams, One Great Game – Football

For the past two years, the New Bern High School football team has played for the state championship. Although they lost both times to a nationally-ranked team from Charlotte, they made us all very proud. But the 2003 and 2004 teams aren't the only ones who have made us proud. Back in the mid-50s, a couple of first-rate coaches made football king here for a while.

Joe Caruso, definitely not to be confused with an opera singer, molded a group of boys from New Bern High into a formidable program. With assistant coach Will Pittman by his side, his teams ruled Kafer Park on Friday nights, rolling out two undefeated seasons.

Some of the players have become Hall of Famers and many of the names are still well known here today: people like the Clement twins (Bob and Joe who played end and tackle), left end Chris Bremmer, right guard Norman Kellum, fullback George Slaughter, team manager Bill Brinkley, and quarterback Bud Parker whose nickname "Preacher Parker" came from the fact that his dad was pastor of First Baptist Church. But alas, as good as these guys were, just like the recent NBHS teams, they fell short both times in their quest for the championship.

The New Bern High football program was primed by a city recreation department program called Midget Football. Today, it is called Junior Football, but at the time it was for seventh and eight graders. If I asked the question, "What football team from North Carolina was the first to play a team from Miami in the Orange Bowl?" most would answer East Carolina, but they'd be wrong.

The New Bern Midget All-Stars were invited to play the Miami Midget All-Stars. The game was the Optimists Boys Bowl and was played on Jan 2, 1949 in the Orange Bowl. On the home side, the citizens of Miami came out in droves to support their team. There to support Bud Parker, Fred Carmichael, Charlie Ashford and Chris Bremmer, along with the other New Bern players, were four people who sat on the visitors' side. One was the bus driver. In the end zone a squadron from the Pensacola Air Station felt so sorry for the "Baby Bears" that they tried to pull them through. New Bern lost 36 to O.

In the mid-50s, there were two high schools in New Bern – one for the white kids and another for the black kids. A thing called separate but equal was enforced throughout most of America. Back then, J.T. Barber was the other school and fortunately the Warriors had a coach that most have said was right on par with Caruso, in all aspects of the game. His name was Simon Coates. With Grover Fields as his assistant, Coates' teams also played for two state championships. In the first one, played against Raleigh in Kafer Park, the Warriors were handily defeated by the visiting team. It seemed that Raleigh had a 300-pound fullback by the name of John Baker, who just bulldozed through the J.T. Barber line at will.

In 1956, Coates again took his team to the state playoff, this time against High Point. When the team got back to New Bern, they brought with them the state championship. Just like the Caruso teams, many of those players are now in the NBHS Hall of Fame. Some of the outstanding players on the team were right end Walt Bellamy, right tackle George E. Brown, center Ed Bell, fullback Ed Mendes, running back William Guion, and quarterback Samuel Whitehurst whose two touchdowns capped the game for the Warriors. As was the case with the Bears, many of the Warriors played on both sides of the ball, referring to themselves as a "60 Minute Man."

In researching this piece I was unable to find all the names from both teams and I really wanted to give credit to all the players. From those teams, many successful men have emerged. Some took advantage of athletic scholarships, some learned what it was like to work with a team, and most learned the self-discipline taught by both coaches.

Today George E. Brown is a retired computer engineer – a football scholarship to North Carolina A&T paved his way.

Like Brown, George Slaughter played for ECU then took his degree and went to work for naval intelligence before retiring back to his hometown. Ed Bell is a retired social worker living in Durham but keeps a second home here. Fred Carmichael is a successful New Bern attorney as is Norman Kellum, who's "With You All the Way." Chris Bremmer is a doctor living in Kinston and Charlie Ashford returned home to practice medicine. Bill Brinkley is a successful CPA.

As for Walt Bellamy, he never made it in football. All he has to his credit is an Olympic Gold medal in basketball and fourteen great years in the NBA. Bud Parker's playing days continued at Wake Forest as starting quarterback. He is now a successful insurance executive. Most Sundays you can find Bud in the choir loft at First Baptist, right behind the pulpit where his father used to preach. Oh yes, and that 300-pound fullback from Raleigh? For the last 30 years or so, he was the sheriff of Wake County.

And what happened to the coaches? Will Pittman still lives here where he retired as superintendent of New Bern schools. Grover Fields was a popular NBHS principal and a middle school bears his name. Caruso and Coates moved on and each Friday night when the Bears tee it up, they do it in a stadium that carries both their names. Those two teams left a positive mark on so many people. But a part of me still wonders how many state championships could have been brought home if those two teams from the 1950s could have played as one.

Charlie

Charlie had been wandering around the golf course for about five days, the greens keeper told my wife.

Lots of people had seen her, but none had stopped to help the ten-year old Cocker Spaniel until Jane picked her up and brought her home.

"How could someone just dump a dog out?" Jane asked when she called me, "especially one that is blind." That day started a relationship that continues to move me.

Charlie was a mess and hungry. After Jane fed her, I took her to the Animal Care Center where she was bathed and clipped. While she was there, they tested her for heartworms. A few days later the phone rang and we were given the bad new, Charlie had heartworms, but a two-pronged treatment might get rid of them. We had no choice; Charlie had to have the treatment.

The treatment for heartworms takes two months and is done in two stages. If, at the end of the first month, the dog has survived the initial treatment, then the second one is given. That survival is a good sign but does not necessarily guarantee that the animal will make it through to a cure.

After her first treatment we took Charlie back to her new home where she was given a bed in the garage and all the dog food she could eat. She had had a pretty eventful first few days and had not yet had the opportunity to explore her new surroundings and meet the rest of her new family: Bob the cat and Thumper, our Pekingese.

I am always amazed at how God looks after his animals. Even though Charlie was blind, it only took her a few days to find her way around her new environment. To watch her negotiate the steps to our deck or roam our fenced-in back yard, an unknowing observer might think she could actually see.

Meeting Bob was quite different, however.

Bob is our male calico Manx, hence his original name. Like most cats Bob is quite curious and kept his distance for a while. One day Charlie bumped into Bob who retaliated with a pop to Charlie's nose. After that, Charlie never forgot Bob's scent and stayed clear when Bob was in the area.

Thumper was another matter. Although he loves people, he tends to be very protective and jealous when it comes to other dogs. When he met Charlie, Thumper wagged his tail and never barked once. I think he knew Charlie was different. They became fast friends.

Life in our back yard became routine for Charlie. Because of his treatment, Charlie slept most of the time and it was necessary to keep her quiet when she was awake. In no time she could tell the difference between Jane and me and would wave her little button of a tail profusely when she heard our voices. Each night before we went to bed, I'd tuck her in and rub her belly until her eyes closed.

After a month it was time for Charlie to have her second treatment. I dropped her off at the veterinary hospital and picked her up the next day. Because she'd made it through the first month, the doctors and I were encouraged.

For the next three weeks nothing changed. Charlie seemed to be on her way to recovery but by the beginning of the fourth week, Jane noticed a difference. Charlie was becoming more and more despondent. A call to Dr. Campbell confirmed our fear. The drug that is used to kill the heartworms was working, but as the heartworms died, they were entering Charlie's lungs and destroying precious tissue. A few days later, Charlie died.

It was a sad time around our house for many weeks. Shortly after Charlie passed on we received a card signed by everyone at the Animal Care Center.

It's been over three years since we had to say goodbye to Charlie and we both still miss her greatly. We only had a little over two months with her and some might ask what difference did an old blind dog make? She reminded me of trust, faithfulness and instant love. That's how Charlie made a difference.

Showdown at the Met

"Oh yes we've got trouble...right here in River City...with a capital T and that rhymes with P and that stands for POOL." With that Robert Preston warned a whole town of the evils of pool in the "Music Man." I wonder if he ever saw the poolroom we had here.

It was called "The Metropolitan Club" and the sign outside said "Billiards," but what it really meant was pocket pool. The front part of the club was a restaurant and probably originated that southern delicacy called the hot hamburger; made up of a slice of bread, two hamburger patties served on a plate topped with French fries, then drenched with brown gravy. I can still hear the cook holler, "'Hot Hamburger' in the back."

The poolroom was in the back and could have easily been the model for the one in the movie "The Hustler." There were two rows of pocket pool tables followed by two snooker tables and the "Joker Poker" table in the corner where many a hardworking soul left his Friday paycheck.

Each table was a full regulation eleven feet, covered with green felt. Above each one, attached to a tin ceiling were Tiffany lamps. Between the lights and the ceiling hung a cloud of blue-gray smoke. Along the walls were elevated seats and benches to allow the kibitzers full view of the action.

Heeding Robert Preston's word, my father told me he'd wear out my behind if he ever caught me in the poolroom, although the restaurant part was okay. That never made sense to me. From age five years old, it was all right to play with Thelma Smith who lived across the street but I couldn't go into her father's place of business. As is with all teenagers, a place off limits was a place of intrigue. I became a regular.

There were some really good pool players back then but the most famous was Wimpy Lassiter from Elizabeth City. He was the national champion. One day after having heard of a pool player from Pollocksville who owned a small gas company, named John D., he and Willie Mosconi, the guy who taught Jackie Gleason to shoot for the movie, came to New Bern to get some of John D's money. Word spread through New Bern High that Friday like measles on a six-year-old. Some guys checked out early to get to the Metropolitan and find a good spot.

When John D. walked into the poolroom that afternoon, Willie and Wimpy were already in the back taking money from some of the young "wannabees." John D. opened his case, screwed together his cue, and the greatest pool game I ever saw began. From that afternoon until late that night balls were racked and re-racked, hundred dollar bills stacked up on the rails and the crowd grew bigger and bigger. When it was all over the hustlers had been out-hustled. Like the fish they were, Willie and Wimpy counted their losses and left without John D's money and most of their own.

We no longer have a downtown poolroom here, but in its "hey day," the Metropolitan Club was as classy as they get. And that pool shooter from Pollocksville? His full name was John D. Jenkins. His little gas company is now one of the largest privately owned gas companies in the United States, and his two daughters, Linda Staunch and Carol Mattocks are well known New Bern residents.

To an impressionable teenager who marveled at seeing a real game of pool that Friday night in the spring of my life, John D., you really made a difference.

The Little Store

Actually there were two "Little Stores" in Trent Woods at one time. The first one wasn't exactly a "Little Store" since it started as a service station but as time progressed, it carried more and more convenience items. (Editor's note: Please notice that I am not referring to convenience stores. That phrase, as it is currently used, had not been coined at the time.)

The filling station was located on the corner of Country Club Road and Wedgewood Drive, right beside the entrance to Country Club Hills. It was built by my father's construction company for Ashford Oil Company, the local Citgo distributor and was very different from most service stations of the day. Its colonial design with long windows and dormers was heavily influenced by the well known New Bern doctor, Charles H. Ashford, Sr., whose wife Caroline and daughter, Tay Roberts are Trent Woods residents.

The reason for the colonial design was that Dr. Ashford was concerned about putting a service station in such an out-of-the-way place. He has been quoted as saying, "Well, if it doesn't make it as a gas station, at least we can sell it as a house." Dr. Ashford's prophecy eventually came true. The building was first converted to a bank and is now the attractive home of the Dunn and Dunn law firm.

The only person that I can remember running the station was Wimpy Barwick. After he sold the Trent Pines Club, he ran the gas station. It was at that time that it became somewhat of a "Little Store." He sold everything from Nabs to fresh produce, including Bogue Sound watermelons.

Just after the Citgo station was built, the other "Little Store" was opened. It was located on Chelsea Road just past the entrance to Matthews Boat Company. Although from the beginning everyone called it the "Little Store," it did in fact have a name. It was called the "Suburban" by its owner Ada Mattox and her husband, both lifelong Trent Woods residents.

Unlike convenience stores of today, the Suburban did not start out selling gas. It opened early and stayed open late, selling all sorts of items from charcoal to ice cream, from soft drinks to dishwashing detergent. It really provided a service. Imagine an old friend popping by at nine in the evening and you had no beer. A quick trip to the Suburban would fix everything.

For the youngsters in Trent Woods, the Suburban offered a place to gather. The older kids had the "Parkway" to go to on summer nights, so the younger ones adopted the Suburban as their place. It became a nightly event to "hang around the 'Little Store'."

The Suburban survived as a "Little Store" for over thirty years but like the Citgo station, it has evolved into another use. Today the Suburban is also an office building.

The demise of the Citgo station and the Suburban left a void in Trent Woods for many years. Not only were they stores of convenience, they were also the hub of our local community. They were places where you would run into almost every resident sometime during the week – places where you could get the scoop on anything that was happening in the town.

Fortunately both stores have been replaced, sort of, but this time their replacement doesn't sell bread and Red Hots. Instead, they sell screwdrivers and paint. I'm talking about the Trent Woods True Value. I reckoned you could call it the unofficial Trent Woods meeting place. Chaz and Bobbie and the boys have their finger on the pulse of the community. At the True Value you can find out everything, from how to change out a toilet seat to who's considering running for town council. And if those guys don't have an answer to your question, all you have to do is wait a few minutes and someone will walk through the front door who will.

I've been told that the more things change, the more they stay the same. But there are many times when a quick trip to the Suburban for ice cream would still add the finishing touch to a slice of apple pie. For over thirty years, at least one of the Trent Woods "Little Stores" made a difference.

Morning Train to the Azalea Festival

"Once upon a time, a girl with moonlight in her eyes, put her hand in mine"….those beautiful lyrics were penned by Lee Adams and accompanied a tune written by Charles Strouse for the Broadway musical "All American"….but hold that thought for just a moment.

Standing on the corner of Hancock and Queen, I'd never seen a locomotive that big. In fact without the distinctive red and yellow paint on the nose, I swore it was an exact replica of the Lionel "Santa Fe" in my train set. Behind the humming diesel were twelve to fourteen passenger cars, a sight I'd only seen in movies or magazines.

The trains that frequented our little town only handled freight. But sitting in front of the depot was an honest-to-goodness passenger train.

A couple of months before, my good friend Dale Goldman had heard about an excursion train that was going to originate in New Bern and travel to Wilmington for the Azalea Festival. At the time, he was dating a girl there, and since at fifteen we couldn't drive, he thought it'd be a great road trip. He even said he could "fix me up."

The train trip excited me but the other part scared me to death. In my mind I pictured Dale spending the day with Miss America while I'd be cuffed to Miss Piggy. But the train adventure won out, even if I had to spend six or eight hours with some 300-pound industrial debutante.

"Come on, we're about to leave," Dale shouted from one of the cars. As soon as I climbed aboard, the conductor – dressed all in dark blue like some character from a TV commercial – shouted "'Board'." With a huge blast from its whistle, the train began to inch its way down Queen Street. Slowly the engine gained speed as we passed through Five

Points and out alongside Park Avenue. By the time we crossed US 17, the cars began to sway back and forth and the clickety-clack of the wheels drummed a rhythm that would inspire an Arlo Guthrie classic.

The excursion, as the trip was billed, started in New Bern and carried both teenagers and parents along with the New Bern High School marching band, which was scheduled to march in the Azalea Festival parade. Along the way the train stopped in Maysville, Jacksonville, Verona, and Holly Ridge to take on more and more festivalgoers and bands. By the time we reached Wilmington, all the cars were full and rocking.

As we approached the Wilmington station, I swallowed hard and checked myself over. If by chance I might be meeting someone I'd like to bring home to mother, I wanted to look okay. That day I wore a burgundy shirt, khaki pants, burgundy socks and, of course, Bass Weejuns. When the train jolted to a stop, Dale and I disembarked and found a huge covered concourse, just like the ones in a World War II movie. As I looked from the door, I saw two girls searching the crowd. "No way," I said to myself. Then my magical journey to Wilmington unfolded. Dale waved at the two girls, and they waved back. I blew into my hands and checked my breath.

Moments later I was introduced to Vickie Alpern. She was my age with brown hair and wide brown eyes; as cute a girl as I'd ever seen. She wore a blue plaid madras dress, cut just above her knees, and Weejuns. Then she reached over and grabbed my hand. In all my life a girl had never reached for my hand first and I blushed. "Come on," she said, tugging on my hand as we ran toward Front Street. "We'll miss the parade."

Today the train tracks to Wilmington are gone and the old New Bern station stands empty, but I'll never forget my first train ride. It was a day when an awkward boy moved closer to becoming a young man. A day of fun that still lingers in my mind. A day when "Once upon a time a girl with moonlight in her eyes, put her hand in mine"…and for one day in my life, made, oh, such a wonderful difference.

Giving Thanks

"Over The River and Through the Woods to Grandmother's House we go" and "Home for the Holidays" sung by Perry Como have always reminded me of Thanksgiving. To the Generation Y'ers that are reading this you probably have no clue what I'm writing about, especially that Como guy. When I grew up, we sang the first one in school and the other was played on the radio. Those songs, along with Thanksgiving officially kicked off the "Holiday" season.

In recent years, at least in my opinion, Thanksgiving has gotten the short end of the stick. All eyes are on Christmas. It's as if we want to get moving toward December 25 faster and faster each year. But to me, Thanksgiving is a day that needs to be savored, not for the turkey and dressing but for the meaning of the day.

The only two countries in the world that officially celebrate Thanksgiving are the United States, on the last Thursday in November and Canada, on the second Monday in October. I get a chill every time I think that these two great nations have set aside a day to give thanks to God for all our blessings.

This year will be a special Thanksgiving for me. Just five weeks ago, my wife, Jane, fell and broke her leg. That fall has created a short-term change in our lives. It has given us both a prospective we've never seen before. For Jane, she will never look at a handicapped person in the same light again. For me, I have grown to appreciate all she did for our family on a daily basis. It has also given me a real understanding of how it must be to be a single parent trying to look after a family and also working for a living. Fortunately for us there is a light at the end of the tunnel and in a few more weeks Jane will be able to walk again. But for many in similar situations that light does not exist.

Jane's injury has also affected me in a different way. All my life, I have been on the giving end when it has come to helping someone out. To be on the receiving end made me very uncomfortable at first. It also made me realize what a loving and giving community we have.

I remember as a child how we all looked after each other by helping our neighbors out when adversity struck; how we'd bring over dinner or pick up groceries for our neighbors. I can tell you now, that at least for us here in this wonderful community, that has not changed.

One night Julia Hudson called over and said, "Skip, I'm bringing supper over whether you want it or not." That night her chicken potpie was a feast for us.

Also the day Ken Gibbs helped me find Bob my cat. Without his direction I still might be out there looking for Bob.

These are just examples of the kindness my neighbors have expressed to us. There are really too many to name, but all of you know who you are.

I'm sure there are other towns in our great nation that have a similar sense of community, but I for one think that what we have in Trent Woods is special. That neighborly feeling that I had growing up still exists.

I hope this Thanksgiving when you thank God for all the blessing He's bestowed upon you and your family that you'll also thank Him for your neighbors, I know that I will. To Jane and I, you've all made a difference.

The Melting Pot

Last Sunday as my wife Jane and I drove home from the jazz showcase, I was unusually quiet, deep in thought. "A penny?" Jane said, her way of asking if I wanted to share my thoughts. To me, thoughts are a very personal thing and oft times I'd rather keep them to myself. But this time was different. "Sure," I said as I turned to Jane. "You know, I really love this town."

New Bern is a very special place. It is a product of many things, foremost a willingness by those of us who've lived here all our lives to accept and welcome those from other places; people who've fallen in love, many at first sight, with our wonderful community. Together we have worked toward the common goal that makes us different from other towns in eastern North Carolina.

I think that difference comes from our heritage. Unlike Kinston, Rocky Mount and Wilson, we have never been tied to tobacco and farming. In New Bern you can't find rows and rows of huge brick houses with slate roofs. There is no old money. We are a trading community. A seaport. Because of that background, strangers have always been welcome here. Those other towns seem to be controlled by cliques who'd just as soon pull in the ladder. I think we reflect the true American melting pot the others are missing.

Of course that openness had to be cultivated. Those of us who have called New Bern home since birth had to look to the future. On the night the Riverfront Convention Center opened, our Lieutenant Governor, someone most of us just call "Bev," was the keynote speaker. That night Governor Perdue talked of a visionary meeting that she had attended some 25 years earlier. During that *Committee of 100* meeting, those in attendance shared their ideas as to what they wanted our community to look like in the next quarter century. The dreams that were set forth seemed impossible at the time. What was envisioned was an industrial park that would accommodate diversified companies. A thriving downtown with shops, restaurants, and bars; hotels and marinas that would rival Annapolis and a convention center that would not only feed off our tourism but help to feed the businesses in downtown. That night Governor Perdue was proud to announce that all of those goals had been achieved. When she finished her speech, the hair on the back of my neck stood up. I had also been at that meeting at the old Holiday Inn and to have ever expected that we could have done so much in such a short time is a real tribute to all of us who live here.

And we continue to be blessed by those who have come to New Bern and fallen in love with what *Sailing Magazine* once called "the best kept secret on the east coast." Our welcome mat has opened the door for some of the most talented folks in all of America. Successful business people, musicians and artists have elected to call New Bern home. Our new citizens don't just sit home. They are involved. Just look at the theater groups, the arts council, Rotary, and Civitan just to name a few. They have not just joined us, they have opened up new and exciting avenues – every time I hear the *Southern Gentlemen* perform I am reminded at what wonderful ambassadors they are.

And there are those who have gone the extra mile to support New Bern. Take John Sturman. For fifteen years, the *Sunday Jazz Showcase* has presented, in sellout performances, some of the greatest jazz musicians in the world – people like Milt Hinton, Kenny Devern and Bobby Rosengarten. Although there are many who make the Showcase possible, it was John's passion for the music and his dream to bring top-quality music to our town that got it all started.

I wonder how many of us start off our day with Phil Knight -- bright and humorous, he is a transplanted Vermonter who hosts *The Daily Neuse Show* each morning from eight until nine, on cable channel 10. His show has grown steadily since it started back in the fall and now at many of the office water coolers people are asking each other if they'd heard what Phil had to say that morning. To say he is opinionated would be a gross understatement. Just listen and you'll quickly find out how he feels. He is especially eager to voice his thoughts on local issues. And if you disagree with him on some subject, just hang around a while and sooner or later he'll bring up a topic that will start your engine.

What both John and Phil share is a love for New Bern. It is not only shown in their actions (Just check out the personalized license plate on the back of John's car. It reads NEW BERN,) it is shown in their involvement in the community. They, along with countless others who recognize what many of us have been aware of for years, have chosen to be a part of this wonderful place we call home.

Yet with all the changes that have taken place, it is nice to know that New Bern has not lost its small town flavor. Yesterday I dropped off my shirts at the cleaners. They didn't ask me how much starch I wanted – they knew. And when I left they didn't give me a pickup ticket. Same thing when I dropped off my shoes at the repair shop. Like John and Phil and so many more, I love this town. Together, we can all continue to make a difference.

Let's Shut Everything Down, It's Snowing

I love snow. I think I've always loved snow. For those of us who grew up in eastern North Carolina, snow was such a rare event that I can't imagine anyone not loving a quiet snowfall. When I was younger, it meant a day off from school. As I grew older, it meant the serenity of a good book and a fire in the fireplace, a reason to take time off and do what I want to do.

We had our first snowfall on January 18th. I'm sure we've probably had other snows since the one at Christmas of 1989, but for some reason I don't remember them. But the first snowfall of the new millennium is one I'll always remember.

My sister was out of town and my wife, Jane, and I had agreed to let her daughter Jenna stay with us. Expecting to take her to school that Tuesday morning, we were all excited to awaken and find the ground covered with more coming down.

After breakfast and morning chores, I noticed the usual crowd gathering at the eighteenth green at New Bern Golf and Country Club. When I was a kid, number eighteen had the biggest hill suitable for sledding in Craven County. There were no bridge overpasses or other manmade structures capable of handling a sled and eighteen was perfect, as long as you didn't wind up in the Trent River.

When Jenna and I got to the top of the hill, we found that most of the regulars were already there: Nancy Deichmann, Missy Taylor, Rob and Ginger Shields, Tommy Faulkenberry, my brother Frank and his wife Dana. But something was different. This time we were not the ones riding the treacherous ice toward the river, it was our kids. A second generation was discovering the hill at number eighteen.

When I was growing up, sleds were not found in the local hardware store as they were in places like Raleigh or Greensboro. It didn't snow here that much and there were really very few hills. For the most part, we used water skis, flying saucers and old Coke signs to negotiate the hill at number eighteen. Someone would always wind up in the river. Things were different this year. Along with the usual aquatic devices, there were two American Flyers, one fairly new and one that belonged to Nancy Deichmann when she was a kid. And to assure a trip into the Trent would not take place; there were now shrubs at the bottom of the hill to provide a perfect stop.

I will never forget the first time I saw an American Flyer sled. One night in December of 1958, it had snowed over 10 inches from the time we went to bed until we got up the next morning. Everything in town shut down and school was closed for four days. On the second day, we discovered the hill at number eighteen and had a ball. Jim Hodges and Stroud Tilley both showed up with American Flyer sleds. Now when you compare sliding down a hill on a garbage can lid to racing down one on an American Flyer – it's like comparing a Model-T to a Corvette. Everyone wanted to ride those sleds.

As the afternoon wore on, we began to seek faster thrills. Stroud noticed that the downriver dock at the Yacht Club was covered in ice. One trial run and we were hooked on the speed. It got to be so much fun that we built a jump near the end and tried to outdistance each other.

Just before dark, Jim Hodges decided to try one more jump…for the record. He started further back from the point of entry to the ice, to gain extra speed. When he hit the slick dock, the sled was laid out perfectly with Jim stretched out on top. As he whizzed toward the jump it looked like Jim was going to make the record. The sled hit the ramp at an incredible speed and Jim soared into the air. The landing was setting up to be a record breaker, but as the right rail hit the dock it found a place that had not been covered with ice. The rail dug into wood and sent Jim flying into the water. Headfirst. At that time I had never seen ABC's Wild World of Sports, but when I finally did, the part about the agony of defeat, when the skier wipes out at the end of the jump, reminded me of Jim Hodges sailing into the river.

We pulled Jim out of the river, along with the American Flyer, and laughed until our sides hurt. None of us were old enough to drive, so Stroud agreed to walk Jim home. Stroud said later that by the time they reached Jim's house on Greenview Road his clothes had frozen on him and made a crackling sound as he walked.

For some reason snow seems prettier in Trent Woods than any other place on earth. Maybe it because it's such a rare treat. But for what it's worth it really makes a difference.

Christmas Downtown

As I drove down Martin Luther King Boulevard last Friday – the busiest shopping day of the year – I was reminded of how much New Bern has changed since I was in high school.

Back then the stretch between Simmons Street and Race Track Road (now Glenburnie) was mostly fields, trees, a railroad crossing and a golf driving range. Today all are gone replaced by the mall, Wal-Mart, Target and various other businesses, car dealerships and restaurants. For the next two weeks, this is where the action will be as shoppers prepare for the big day on December 25th. But there was a time when all that action took place in the four-block area we call downtown.

As I look back in my mind's eye I still see what New Bern looked like those thirty-some years ago. Middle Street was dominated by the big department stores. Belk, Penney's, and Montgomery Ward anchored Middle Street, each festively decorated, trying to mimic a Macy's or a Sax's and, in many ways, succeeding. Smaller department stores like the Charles Store, Lipman's and Copeland-Smith helped to carry the season's theme only to be followed up by specialty shops like Hill's, The Fashion Center, The Parisian and Bryant-McLeod, just to name a few.

Back then the stores pulled out all the stops to look Christmasy. Some even had animated windows with snowmen or Santas that whirled around and danced back and forth with elves and fairies.

And the city did its part too. By today's standards, those multi-colored lights strung between light poles, covered in something that looked an awful lot like moss, seemed more like something Chevy Chase would have hung, but to me they looked pretty good. By the week before Christmas, downtown with its throngs of people, and festive mood resembled a small Fifth Avenue.

The one thing that still makes me smile was the mood of the shoppers. By the time I reached my senior year at New Bern High, I had a Saturday job in the shoe department at Belk's. Obviously it carried over to the Christmas season. I loved selling shoes, especially to girls, and I think I learned more about marketing in that shoe department than any college course I ever took. However, the thing I remember most about working in Belk's that year was how pleasant the shoppers were. Everyone seemed to understand the meaning of Christmas. I can still feel the warmth of the smiles and the greetings, both inside the store and on the sidewalk. That really put me into the spirit of why we were there in the first place.

There were also two events that I looked forward to during the Christmas season. One was the annual New Bern High School Choir's Christmas concert. It was an event that my family never missed. The boys' and girls' glee clubs performed first, followed by the A Cappella Choir, each group bringing both popular and religious music to the audience, all under the masterful direction of Donald Smith, one of the most demanding and musically talented people I have ever known.

The other event, started long before I was born and ended before I entered New Bern High. It was called the Yuletide Review and was combination Christmas pageant and variety show. The show was the brainchild of a real New Bern character by the name of J. Gaskill McDaniel. McDaniel, I'm told, never drove a car. He was a newspaperman who really chronicled our community, first working as a correspondent for a Raleigh paper, then as publisher of his own weekly, *The New Bern Mirror*. The thing I liked best about his paper were the photographs of high school girls in bathing suits, taken by well known New Bern photographer Billy Benners, that appeared each week on the back page.

I'm told that the first show took place at the Masonic Theater and started at 11 p.m., after the final movie. The first time I saw the "Review," it took place at the Shrine Auditorium then was later moved to the NBHS auditorium. Joe, as all his friends called him, emceed the show in a fashion akin to Ed

Sullivan, introducing acts that each year led up to the finale which featured the NBHS Choir leading the audience in singing "Silent Night."

After twenty-five years, Joe McDaniel called it a night and brought the review to a close. Shortly after that, Donald Smith moved on to a college position and the glory days of the Choir and Glee Club were gone. Then the face of downtown changed. All the old stores have either closed or moved. But when I shop this year, most of it will still take place in downtown. Now we have some of the best specialty shops around and it's also easy to find a place to park. And for some reason, there are still those smiling faces and Christmas greetings that did not leave. Merry Christmas.

The Music Man

Friday night was one of those special times that will forever be engraved in my brain. I was one of the fortunate ones to have had the opportunity to sing in a choir made up of former students from the New Bern High School choral department. We came together to surprise our former director, Donald Smith, who had been at the high school from 1940 until 1964.

The whole idea was started when the class of 1954, the last class to graduate when the high school was located in the Griffin Building on Hancock Street, decided that along with their 50th anniversary, they would host a reception on the Friday night before their reunion. The reception was for anyone who'd ever graduated from the old school. Since Donald Smith had been invited as the special guest for the weekend, it seemed only appropriate that a choir be put together to sing for him.

Back in February, John Mason, the class president, put out the word asking anyone who'd ever sung in one of Mr. Smith's choirs to meet at First Baptist Church in order that a reunion choir be re-created. That night more than 50 of Mr. Smith's former students set off on a journey that – to me – has been unforgettable. For the next four months, the Donald Smith Reunion Choir, under the direction of the current NBHS choir director, B.J. Oglesby, sharpened our skills, aiming for the grand surprise. Talk about commitment! We had singers coming every other week, then every week from as far away as Raleigh and Wilson – representing classes from 1947 – 1965.

To have B.J. Oglesby as our director was a coup made possible by Mason and fellow choir member Bud Parker. The similarities between B.J. and Smith are almost eerie. Not only does she direct the choral department at the high school but she is also the choir director at First Baptist Church, a job Smith held for much of his tenure in New Bern. And the similarities don't stop there. She is as good a musician as I have ever known – both demanding and instructive. She expected the choir to give its very best for our former teacher. B.J. took those aging jewels, so finely crafted by Smith many years before, and polished the choir until we sparkled.

After one particularly tough rehearsal, I heard a couple remark as we were leaving the building that "I think B.J.'s got a little Donald Smith in her."

I think that I speak for all the choir members in thanking her for a job well done.

When Smith was choral director, things were a lot different than they are today. It was a time when the music department stood toe-to-toe with the athletic department. In fact, it was a time when most athletes stood in line to make it to one of Smith's choirs. Like the legendary football coach, Joe Caruso, Smith taught discipline and self-respect. And like Caruso's teams, the choirs won competition after competition.

Today, arts-related subjects seem to suffer more than other programs in the schools. Things like creative writing, painting, music, and dance usually take a backseat to football and basketball.

Just last month, B.J. took her choir to a regional competition. It took place at Paramount's King's Dominion, where the NBHS choir competed against 115 choirs from schools representing eight different states. When the competition was over, I'm proud to announce that the NBHS choir took home the first place award, yet no news organization picked it up. In Smith's days that item would have been front-page news.

When the evening was over, I think all of us who worked so hard to perform for our old teacher felt a sense of well being. How many times in your life can you say that you were a part of a real life "Mr. Holland's Opus?" To paraphrase George Bailey from "It's a Wonderful Life," the judge of a man's worth is in his friends. Donald Smith, I think on Friday night, you saw how much you're thought of in New Bern. Thanks for the memories and thank you for making a difference.

The Christmas Puppy

The first time I met Thumper was in February of 1987. If it hadn't been for my wife Jane, it would have been our one and only meeting. The night before, we had taken my mother and one of her friends to Chapel Hill to see a basketball game. For those of you who know me, that was like asking me to sit through a paint-drying contest. I think I got bored with basketball after Dean Smith failed in his umpteenth try to win a national championship. But accommodating my mother was more important than any old round ball game.

On our way back home – please understand that I was traveling with three women and a direct route from UNC to home was impossible – we stopped at the Cary Village Mall. Shortly after the ladies went inside, I finished the book I was reading and decided to buy some work boots. Upon finishing my purchase, I wandered into the pet store that was next door. I'm a real sucker for pet stores and the first thing I went to was the section with the puppies. That's when I first saw him curled up in a cage – all white and tan and furry and lonely. But there was something wrong. He was twice as big as the other Pekingese puppies. "Why's he so large?" I asked the clerk. Being a good sales person, she quickly unlocked his cage and placed him in my arms. "He was a Christmas puppy," she said. "We sold him three times before Christmas but each time the buyers' credit failed, so we've just had to keep him. Now he's older and bigger than the others, and I believe a little depressed about being in his cage for so long." The little boy seemed so shy as I held him, unlike most others who wag their tails and lick and lick. He just stared at me with those big, sad eyes

"What have you got there?" I heard over my shoulder as Jane walked up beside me. "He's so cute," she said as she held out her hand to pet him. "Why's he so big?" After I told her the story she wanted to know if we were going to take him home. When I explained that we already had Buffy, our little Peke, at home and that we really didn't need another dog, along with a hundred more excuses, she turned and walked away. As I handed Thumper back to the clerk, one of his paws hung to my sweater as if he didn't want to let go. I must admit it was hard to watch him go back into his cage.

On the way home, it was quiet in the front seat. Jane sat there looking out at the side of the road. And my thoughts were also back at the pet store. But neither of us spoke about it then. That night as we were finishing dinner, Jane looked at me as a tear slipped down her cheek. "If I can figure a way to get to the Cary Village Mall, I'm going back tomorrow and buy that dog."

And that's what she did. Knowing that she has never been good at directions, her father found Jane a driver, and by dinner the next night our new Christmas Puppy was at his new home. Before long he became a regular member of our family, bonding with Buffy and even learning to catch a ball in the air and to throw it back – something he has never tired of.

As I write this column, my little boy is sprawled across my lap. Every now and then he raises his head, yawns, and looks at me with his bright black eyes. I guess it's his way of knowing that everything is all right. He's older now and instead of charging across the kitchen floor when I come home at night he now ambles toward me, his tail wagging a little slower, but his bark is as hardy as ever. This Christmas will be a special one for Thumper and for us. It will be his sixteenth. That puts him a little over a hundred years old in human terms. The chance he'll see another holiday season is pretty slim and the thought of him not being with us is something I cannot quite fathom. To imagine an empty lap as I write is as impossible as missing that bark that has always announced my arrival. And the thought of having to put his ball away for good blasts an infinite hole through my heart. Thumper may have spent his first Christmas without a family, but for Jane and me, we're so glad that he waited for us to find him that February day so that we could spend the next 15 Christmases together. To us he'll always be our Christmas Puppy.

Welcome Nobles

For years, during Christmas, the city stretched a sign across Broad Street at the Middle Street intersection. It was made up of 14 round lights about the size of a large hubcap, each illuminated with a letter that spelled "Merry Christmas." By mid-January, as if by magic, the sign changed to "Welcome Nobles," announcing that the Shriners were coming to town.

Each year from as far back as I can remember, the Shriners of the Sudan Temple have converged on New Bern in January for their Winter Ceremonial. It is this time that they gather to have fun and to elect and install a new Potentate.

The Sudan Temple is one of the largest Shrine organizations in the state. It is comprised of 42 clubs that cover what is considered eastern North Carolina.

These fun loving guys have always put on one whale of a parade, but when I was in high school it had to have been the best in the state. I know – I helped put it on.

Back then, the parade was held on Friday morning and for some reason, only the band and a bunch of pretty girls were able to leave school for the parade. Why we had to miss such an event troubled me. Then one day I became a part of the parade. My scoutmaster, Charlie Taylor, had been selected as the Parade Chairman and needed help in lining up the floats, bands and participants. In those days, the parade made up at Kafer Park on Queen Street. From there it followed the traditional route, down Broad to Middle, then to South Front, up Craven, ending at the Temple where a huge feed was provided to all the participants.

Besides units from the different Shrine clubs, there were floats with girls dressed in furs and long gowns and marching bands. In those days, most clubs paid the transportation costs to have the respective high school bands in attendance. We're talking about 15 to 20 bands, at least.

As the parade lined up, each marching unit took a position at the end of George Street where it changed its name to National Avenue. The floats were stacked into the old ballpark. Along both sides of the street the different Shrine Club units set up. It was my job to coordinate the floats and the bands. Like a Vegas dealer, I shuffled them together as the parade moved forward.

The pre-parade atmosphere was circus-like. While the bands tuned up, drummers practiced their cadences and majorettes strutted and twirled. One unforgettable pair of Shriners took advantage of the organized chaos and had a little fun. These guys had an open car, either an old Ford or Chevy. They would find unsuspecting participants, usually band members or sideline watchers, and ask them to go for a ride. After settling in the back seat, the unsuspecting quarry would vault from the car, shouting and laughing. It seemed that the buttons on the seat covers were electrically charged and once the riders had been comfortably seated, the driver would send a shock into the back seat.

Once underway, the Shriners were the stars. The Sudan Marching Patrol led off, followed by convertibles full of dignitaries, including the outgoing and incoming Potentates. Strategically placed in between the bands and the floats were the visiting Shrine units, each with their own theme. There were Clowns from Dunn, Keystone Cops out of Jacksonville, Chanters, Calliopes and lots and lots of funny little vehicles driven by grown men. One year, members of the Carteret County Shrine Club came dressed as duck hunters. They had two motorized duck boats and fired shotguns that exploded into fireworks high above the downtown skyline.

But one troupe of characters will always stand out. I think they were called the Oriental Band. This band, paying flutes and clanging cymbals was led by a guy wearing bloomer-type pants, pointed shoes that curved back toward his ankles, all the while directing his men with a scimitar-type sword. Even on the coldest winter day, he never wore a shirt – his huge belly dangling over the sash that struggled to hold up his pants. Every so often he'd stop in front of a gang of parade watchers and jiggle that belly back and forth and up and down, making it do things an exotic dancer would envy.

Today, most of the bands and floats are gone. The parade has been moved to Saturday where we can all enjoy the antics of some of those same Shrine units. And like in past years, the Shriners still stroll Middle Street wearing those funny little red hats and saying "Hi Noble" to one another. But I am reminded that besides their fun side they play a very important part in our lives. Nationwide, they run 22 hospitals dedicated to orthopedics and burn treatment. Today, because of the Shriners, more than 400 of our neighbors, right here in eastern North Carolina, are benefiting from specialized medical care. So this weekend when you see one of our Shriner guests, how about giving them a big New Bern welcome and thank them for making a real difference in our lives.

You and "Me" need a Dog to Ski

Pretty soon the jet skis will be cranking up in the Trent River. On a calm day you can hear them all the way over to Bellefern. These powerful water motorcycles are all the thing now, and I can confess that I have had some fun jumping wakes and spinning circles in one. But anyone can ride them. Years ago it took skill to enjoy the rage at the time. That was water skiing.

Water skis were preceded by aqua planes. The best way to describe the thing is to say that it looked like a piece of plywood that was warped at the top. Attached to the leading edge was a rope that was tied to a boat which pulled the device along. The rider crouched on top of the board, and once it began to plane, would stand up and hold on to the aqua plane by another rope that had been tied to the board. The only maneuvering that took place was decided by the helmsman of the boat that pulled the thing. Mainly the rider was just along for the ride.

Then someone invented the water ski. First as a pair, then a single called a slalom. Water skiing changed everything. Since the skis were attached only to the riders' (skiers') feet, and not directly to the boat, the water skier had complete mobility and freedom, at least within the perimeters set forth by the length of the towrope.

Skiers could now crisscross the boat's wake, jump those same wakes as well as those of other passing boats. They could zoom past docks and spray the sunbathers, a really fun thing that I liked to do.

I first learned to ski by taking lessons from a qualified water ski instructor. My dad decided that it would be better to learn the technique properly rather than to drown behind someone's boat as I was hauled up and down the river.

He was right. I met Wimpy Barwick at the Trent Pines Club one Saturday morning in early June. Wimpy and his wife ran the club, which was a fun summer place, dedicated to river activities, especially water skiing. Wimpy took me to the water's edge and showed me the proper way to put on the skis. He then showed me, while still on the beach, the proper way to rise out of the water. He placed a ski rope handle in my hands then pulled against it, allowing me to get a feel of how the boat would pull me up, which was the most important part of taking off. He told me to keep my back straight, keep my arms straight in front of me and to let the boat do the work.

When it was time for my first try, Wimpy's wife pulled their black inboard speedboat in close to shore and panned out a ski rope. I was already in the water with my skis on. Wimpy met me in the water with his skis on as well. In his hand was what looked like a ten foot long ski handle, which he attached to the towrope. Wimpy told me that we would be skiing together, both holding on to the long handle. I felt safe. My coach was right beside me.

We started from shallow water. Wimpy told me that the worst thing anyone could do when learning to ski was to start in deep water. In shallow water, the student didn't have to waste energy treading water.

When I was ready, my instructor told me to tell the boat to go. I yelled, "Hit it," and the big inboard lunged forward. I could see Wimpy out of the corner of my eye. He'd told me not to stand up until he gave the word. I could feel the skis flying along as I sat in the crouched position, back straight and arms outstretched. Then I heard him, "Stand up," he shouted. I stood up, and I was skiing. In those days, to say that you'd gotten up on the first try was a badge of accomplishment. Thanks to my dad and Wimpy Barwick, I'd done it.

After a couple of turns around the river in front of the club, Mrs. Barwick brought the boat in close to shore and slung us into the same beach where we had started. The rest of the day I spent skiing by myself.

After learning to ski on two skis, the slalom was next, then a few tries at the ski jump. I found the jump a little treacherous, and since I was in no mood to break a leg, I let that experience go. I also never learned to ski barefooted, although I drove Hunt Baxter's boat the first time he ever did it. Hunt accomplished a great deal before his untimely passing, but I will forever be in awe of him for that feat.

Like most kids my age, I couldn't get enough. Water skiing became my passion. Most of the time, the biggest problem was getting hold of a towboat. My friends George and Scrappy Bell had a Matthews duck boat, built right here in New Bern by Bobby Matthews. It was about 12 feet long and had an Evinrude seven and a half on the back. When they suggested we try to ski behind their boat, I thought we would spend a lot of time dragging each other around the river. None of us had ever seen anyone water ski behind a boat with less than an eighteen-horse power engine.

For a while our experiment seemed to tell us our original gut reaction was right. We spent a lot of time drinking river water. The boat just wouldn't plane, and without that, it is impossible to get a skier up. Then one of us had an idea. If we could get just the right weight in the bow of the boat, maybe it would plane.

The Bell's Labrador retriever was just about the right weight, so we placed him in the bow. George gunned the motor and all of a sudden the boat planed and I came up out of the water. What a sight that was, a duck boat with a seven and a half, pulling a skier with a black Lab sitting in the bow. From then on all we needed to go water skiing was a tank of gas and George and Scrappy's dog. That whole summer, to a bunch of 10 and 11 year-old-boys, that dog really made a difference.

Bermuda – The Trip of a Lifetime

Most people who know me know that for over 18 years, my passion was sailing. Not just sailing but sailboat racing. I spent over 40 weekends a year on the Neuse River and the Atlantic Ocean, doing exactly what I loved.

There was the spring series, the fall series, and best of all the frostbite series, sailed out of Fairfield Harbour on eight weekends, starting in October and ending in February. That's where the cream of the crop from all the clubs in the state met to show off their skills.

During those winter races, we would have the best of the best come from Wilmington, Oriental, Bath, Little Washington, Beaufort and Morehead City. The competition was awesome.

Like anything else, learning to race took time and study. The first year or two I spent most of my time sucking around at the back of the pack. Then over the winter, one year, I read a book by Arthur Knapp, called "Race Your Boat Right." The next spring the stuff I learned from that book was placed into practical application, and Mr. Knapp brought me from the back to the front. But it was not until I learned to have fun that I stayed at the front for most of the rest of my career.

Until racing became fun, it was more like a job. If we'd done badly on a particular Sunday, I'd carry the loss through the following weeks until getting a chance to redeem myself with the next race. One day, I said to myself, "This is no fun. What am I trying to prove?" That realization made the biggest difference in my racing. Once I started to have fun and set my ego aside, I started to win consistently. No more did I worry about mistakes, but just took them as they came. The last nine years were the most productive and the most fun. Experience had taught me how to race, setting my personal pride aside had taught me how to have good time doing it.

During those racing years, I had an opportunity of a lifetime. A group of guys, mostly from Trent Woods, met each morning for breakfast at Williams Restaurant in downtown New Bern. You know the one "Known from Maine to Florida." Well, it just so happened that Fred Woodruff had just bought this magnificent Morgan 41sailboat. It was just perfect for a blue water voyage. It was kind of like in an old Mickey Rooney – Judy Garland musical. "Hey guys, my dad's got this old barn and we could put on a show." Fred had this new boat and we could sail her to Bermuda. So we did.

After much preparation, on June 10, 1978 the sailing yacht *Kristen* cast off from dock at the Sanitary Seafood Market and Restaurant in Morehead City and set sail for Hamilton, Bermuda. On board were Fred, Rex Wills, Charlie Gryb, John Ward, Bill Rawls, Jim O'Daniel, Jeffery Dick and myself. Donald Andrews, Cooper Kunkel, and Bill Brinkley joined the boat in Bermuda and relieved some of the crew for the return trip. All but Jeffery Dick were Trent Woods residents.

The boat was as well equipped as any I've sailed on. We had more electronics than a surveillance ship. For four and a half days, we sailed to Bermuda and never pulled the boom over. We ate three meals a day and dined at suppertime, wine included. We even still had ice in the fridge when we docked at the Royal Bermuda Yacht Club.

Two days after we arrived in Bermuda, the return crew and our wives met us, and for the next week twelve couples mostly from Trent Woods, played and ate our way around the islands. It was the trip of a lifetime.

There are many other stories about that trip to Bermuda that I'll save for another time. Some, however, can only be told by word of mouth, since they are not appropriate for a family newspaper.

I've often said that the best four years of my life were the ones I spent in college. I can also say without a shadow of a doubt that the best four days of my life were spent in the early part of June of 1978 sailing to Bermuda with that great group of guys.

Editor's Note

In the spring of 2004, Fred Woodruff passed away, a finer man I have never known.

Farewell my captain.

Will the Last Person to leave Kinston, Turn Out the Lights

The noise was deafening. Bears coach, Bob Lewis had called time out with one second left on the clock. Over in the far corner of the gym, the legendary Paul Jones went over the final defensive call with his Kinston Red Devils. When the horn sounded ending the time out, the Devils took up positions at the far end of the court. There was no one to hassle the inbound pass. Like 1-800- PIN DROP, the New Bern High Gymnasium, filled beyond fire code, fell silent. On both sides cheerleaders hugged each other and held their breath.

When the referee passed the ball to forward Eugene Long, center Bill Bunting broke for mid-court. Long heaved the ball high in the air toward his friend. Bunting met the ball in midair and, in a move even Michael Jordan would have been proud of, sent it sailing toward the visitors' goal. Like in a slow motion movie, the ball floated closer to the hoop. Hearts pounded and palms sweated. As the buzzer sounded, the ball reached the top of its arc and started downward. When it found nothing but net, the New Bern fans erupted. We had beaten archrival Kinston by one point, for the conference championship.

The year was 1965 and that greatest of all time New Bern basketball team met Kinston two more times; once in the conference tournament and then finally they played in Durham again – for the state championship. Alas, we lost both times.

The rivalry between the two schools is really one between two towns, each as different as their names suggest – one town based on farming, the other on tourism and trade.

During the '50s and '60s, the competition between New

Bern and Kinston was as heated as any in the state. Whenever a new industry or business looked at eastern North Carolina, it seemed to always boil down to New Bern versus Kinston. The other coastal communities all had some sort of basis on which to build. Greenville had ECU, Goldsboro had the Air Force, and Jacksonville, the Marines. And although Kinston had a small share of the tobacco market, as did Greenville, it did not measure up to Rocky Mount and Wilson.

Even when Tryon Palace opened, Kinston tried to get a share of our tourist business by playing off some old piece of rotten wood, half buried in the Neuse River, called the CSA Ram "Neuse." Give me a break. The only time I saw it, it was hard to tell it had ever been a part of a tree, let alone a boat.

Since that famous basketball game in 1965, much has changed. For some reason, several years ago, the powers that be in Kinston decided to pull in the ladder and we decided to move forward. Today the "Flower of the East" lies just thirty-six miles southeast of Kinston. For years we called New Bern "The Land of Enchanting Waters" yet little was done to promote that asset. Today our downtown bustles with restaurants and bars and shops. The historic district not only exceeds Beaufort and Bath, it equals Williamsburg. Instead of a place for a tourist day trip or bus stop, New Bern has become a favorite stopover. Not only are there things to see, but things to do.

While Kinston chose to stand still, hotels, banks and businesses have replaced the warehouses and wharves of downtown New Bern. Our leaders looked ahead to make sure that roads, schools and infrastructure would keep pace with the steady growth that we've sought. And one trip to our wonderful town and its bedroom communities this time of year, with flowers that challenge Augusta and Wilmington, is enough to know why we're considered one of the best retirement communities in the nation.

Today Kinston is trying to catch up, but it's a long way from first gear to fourth especially when sitting still is the same as backing up. I'm told that things are so slow over there that the Maytag repairman is not the loneliest guy in town anymore, it's the real estate agent.

That conference championship game our boys won some thirty-seven years ago might have been a premonition of things to come. Although we lost to Kinston in the state playoffs, one thing is for sure – as far as both communities are concerned, we've never lost to them since.

Teachers

Of all the people who touch our lives, we probably owe the most to teachers. As I think back on the ones that touched me most, they are the teachers who taught me something that I carried forth, not only in school but also in life.

I started school at Eleanor Marshall School in the Ghent area. My first grade teacher was Mrs. Haslett. Most of the school she taught in was torn down a few years ago but her lovely brick home that was next door is still there and the home of my friend Suzanne Kelly and her family. Mrs. Haslett placed me in the "yellow birds" reading class and taught me the alphabet and how to read.

My second grade teacher was Liz Sumrell. One day during a "tiptoe" recess, I approached Mrs. Sumrell in the hall, lifted up my leg and told her to "kiss my foot." I was abruptly escorted in to see Mr. Flowers, the principal. Mrs. Sumrell taught me the fear of going to the principal's office, a place I would avoid for the rest of my career. She also taught me to respect my teachers. When they tore down the school, Mrs. Sumrell recovered one of the bricks, embroidered "EMC" on it and gave it to me. It's used as a doorstop in my house.

Mrs. Smithwick was my third grade teacher. When I flunked my first Weekly Reader test, my parents were called in for a consultation. Along with my parents' help, I learned the meaning of comprehension. Mrs. Smithwick taught me that although I knew how to read, I needed to understand what I read.

The sixth grade brought Mrs. DuPree, considered the hardest teacher at EMS. Her nickname was Mrs. Do-Hard. What I learned from her was that there was more to school than just math and history. I found out that I could get an "A" from drawing. She introduced me to art.

The seventh and eighth grades probably were the hardest on me. Going through puberty was the worst time of my school life, but fortunately I had Marjorie Rice, who still lives in the New Bern area and Mrs. Willis. By the grace of God and those two teachers, I made it to high school.

At New Bern High, things were different. For the first time, all the preparation began to make sense. I hated algebra but in Mrs. Bynum's geometry class I found out it had a practical use. Johnnie Green showed me that there was no such phrase as "a purple lady's pocketbook," unless of course if the lady was purple. Mrs. Fillmore introduced me to modern literature and Jimmy Smith made physics interesting. And Donald Smith taught me to sing.

During high school, I found out that the learning process could also be fun. As a teenager, most activities centered around the school. In the fall there were football games and sock hops. The winter brought on basketball and in the spring the prom highlighted the end of the school year. There were band concerts and choir concerts, science fairs and study hall. And making interaction with each other was something we'd take with us through life.

College was an even greater learning experience. Those of you who know me, especially when it comes to football, know that when I bleed, it's usually purple, for my adopted ECU. But the four years I spent in Chapel Hill were the most rewarding of my life. There were so many things to learn and do. The outstanding professors were many, however, one stands out. His name was Dr. Frank Ryan.

Dr. Ryan taught American history. As with many UNC professors, he was just a little left of Marx and Lenin. At the time I took his class, the war in Vietnam was raging and as a senior, I was preparing to graduate and do my patriotic duty. Dr. Ryan and I could not have been more divided on the war. Many times during his class, he and I discussed our opposing views. But unlike the discussions held in the schoolyard, ours were civil. When I made a point he'd say, "I must think about that," and when he made a point he'd tell me, "You must think about that."

I'm afraid there are no true liberals left; those who examine all points of view before making up their minds. Today they just shout their opinions at you. But Dr. Ryan was a true liberal, one who used objectivity in his thinking. Although we disagreed, he never held my opinions against me. I earned an "A" in his class. More than American history, Dr. Ryan taught me to listen to people who have a different point of view because sometimes we can learn something that might affect our own opinion.

To single out one teacher in my life would be difficult, although Dr. Ryan would surely be seated at the head of the class. Learning is a progression, from learning to read to learning to listen. I am sure of one thing; there are several teachers in your life that made a difference.

Remembering Jives Fisher

The room was light and airy, but on most days a layer of blue smoke hung just below the metal ceiling. On the right side there were five barber chairs and on the left seats for as many as 10 to 12 patrons. Between each waiting client stood a combination magazine rack/ash tray and at both ends dull copper spittoons sat on the floor. At the far end a shoeshine stand made room for two at a time. Beside the window that looked out onto Broad Street with the name "Service Barber Shop" neatly painted in white and red letters, a striped barber pole rotated endlessly toward the sky.

In the mid to late 1960s Service Barber Shop was the largest in New Bern, a hangout for both men and teenagers. The smell was that of tobacco, shoe polish and Witch Hazel and the conversation tended to dwell mostly on sports and politics. The magazines were always those that men liked to read; ones like *Argosy, Field and Stream, Yachting, Popular Mechanics*, and *Esquire* (a little less notorious than in earlier days).

As is likely to be the case when men get together, there was always a little wagering that took place, especially at the Coke machine that stood in the far left corner by the back door. No two people I ever saw bought a Coke without "Traveling." Embossed on the bottom of each bottle was the name of the town where the drink had been bottled. Wagers were placed on which bottle came from the furthermost point. For some reason mine always had "New Bern" on the bottom.

Those were the days, when men cut men's hair and a style or a "do" took place at a salon. Mac McCausley was my barber from the first time he placed me in a booster seat atop his chair and cut my hair while I screamed at my father. He continued as my barber until he retired in the late '60s. Haircuts were not all they did at Service Barber Shop. Just like in an Al Capone movie, patrons could sit in the chairs draped in a stripped cover with their feet propped up as a man shined their shoes and the barber gave them a shave, a facial and a haircut.

At the rear of the shop a man by the name of Fredrick Melvin Fisher, held court. Jives, as he was known to everyone, ran the shoeshine stand. Crippled with polio as a child, he hobbled around on a platform shoe shining shoes and keeping the shop clean. Jives knew more about baseball than any person I have ever known, before and since. And he also knew about shoes. When a bunch of us guys didn't want to give up our brown Weejun loafers to wear with our prom tuxedos, Jives devised a way to temporarily dye them black. By the time we got to the beach the next day, the brown color had come back.

Jives could also make a pair of shoes shine like they were made out of glass. His secret was a bottle of white liquid that he applied to the toe of the shoe just before he popped the final rag. Last month Gordon Clark, whose mother owned the building, shared that secret with me. He'd promised Jives that he'd never divulge it until after his death. I think I might keep that promise too.

Jives was a devout Catholic and he and his wife Anna raised eight children. According to his oldest son Rick, the director of the Craven Diagnostic Center, Fisher and his wife set the bar high for their kids, something they're all thankful for today. He also was a man of uncommon wisdom, and many a young man, both black and white sought his counsel. His passing in 1971 left a hole in our community.

Although I do miss the smell of tonic and the sound of a ringing spittoon, I do have to admit that today I feel pampered when Debbie Roberts, at Ann's Hair Designs, washes and cuts my hair. Gone are the *Field and Stream* and *Popular Mechanics* magazines, replaced by *Cosmo* and *Glamour*. Gone are the hum of electric clippers and the slapping of a straight razor against a leather strap. But at least we can still talk sports. Debbie knows more about NASCAR than any guy I know. At least some things don't change, thank goodness, and memories continue to make a difference.

* * *

Today there is still a Service Barbershop in New Bern. The barbershop in the above article was in a different location at a different time and under a different ownership. Carlton, the current owner, and his guys still cut hair the old-fashioned way and carry on a lot of the traditions of the old Service Barber Shop that was downtown. I'm told you can still find a copy of *Field and Stream* there.

A Christmas Story

When I arrived at work the morning of December twenty-third in 1997, I was both mentally and physically exhausted. I felt that I had lost the meaning of Christmas.

Christmas had become one thirty-day rush hour driven at a maddening pace. What used to be a fun time for me was one full of seventeen-hour days that began at six-thirty in the morning and ended at eleven-thirty at night. The small pleasures of life like reading the Sunday paper and watching the evening news were done while wrapping or decorating. As the ad on TV said, "there's no time for relaxing, we've gotta do some waxing."

As I often do, I decided to put my feelings down on paper so that maybe I could come to grips with them. The result was a piece called "Where Is Christmas?" Some have called it a poem, although it has neither rhyme nor iambic pentameter. Others have called it an essay. I call it a letter to my soul.

When I finished my little piece, it renewed my understanding of the meaning of Christmas. I felt so good about it that I called a friend and shared it with her. My friend cried after I read it to her and insisted that I send the work to the *Sun Journal*.

At first I resisted, thinking that it was just something to be shared with friends and family, but my friend continued insisting so I promised her that I'd call John Graham, who was the publisher of the paper and read it to him. After he heard my piece, John paused for a moment, then asked me to bring him a written copy. He said he wanted to print it the next day.

On Christmas Eve morning, I opened the *Sun Journal* and turned to the editorial page. I found a reprint of the famous *New York Sun* editorial, "Yes Virginia, There is a Santa Claus."

It was being reprinted on its one-hundredth anniversary. On the opposite page I found "Where is Christmas?" It was the first time anything I'd written had been published.

My friend passed away three Decembers ago. Had it not been for her encouragement it would have been several more years before I'd see any of my articles in print. She really loved Christmas and made a difference in so many lives. Thank you my Weezer, this one's for you.

Where is Christmas
By Skip Crayton
December 23, 1997

Yes, Virginia, there is a Santa Claus, but where is Christmas?

You can find Santa at the mall, on Middle Street, and even on television.

Yes, Virginia, there is a Santa Claus, but where is Christmas?

People rush to and fro at a frantic pace to buy toys and gifts so that Santa can place them under the tree on Christmas Day.

Mothers and dads hit the malls the day after Thanksgiving to run up huge excesses on their credit cards.

Yes, Virginia, there is a Santa Claus, but where is Christmas?

For weeks, we give up our favorite pastimes like reading the Sunday paper or watching the evening news to wrap presents or string those confounded lights that never seem to work in unison.

Yes, Virginia, there is a Santa Claus, but where is Christmas?

Traffic jams and road rage fill the streets around our favorite shopping spots.

Moms and dads tempers flare for not having enough time, only to collapse with exhaustion on Christmas afternoon.

But Virginia, if you'll just look around, you'll discover that you can find Christmas.

It's in the Sun Journal's Empty Stocking Fund. The TV 12 food drive, and the Marine Corps' Toys for Tots. It's in the Salvation Army's bell-ringers.

And you can find it at First Baptist's candlelight service and Centenary's live nativity scene.

It can even be seen on television where George Bailey taught us that it is truly a "Wonderful Life."

Yes, Virginia, there is a Santa Claus, but more important, at least in Craven County, there is a Christmas.

Dreams

When I think of May, I usually think of graduation day. That's the one day that we can all remember. It marks a milestone in our lives.

For some, graduation marks the end of a long educational process, be it from high school or from college. For others, it means just another step in a process that will sooner or later eventually end at a final graduation day.

When that time comes, whether it is from high school or medical school, we all will join the work force. For many that will mean applying the training received in school. For others it will be just trying to get a job; one that will at least pay the bills.

I've always wanted to give a commencement address. I guess to do so I'd have to be famous or a real community mover and shaker. More than likely that address before my high school or college alma mater will not happen. But because of the forum that the newspaper gives me, I would like to take this opportunity to share with you some of those thoughts I'd like to tell a new group of graduating seniors.

Graduation is a fork in the road. It is a time to make decisions. If there is one idea I'd like to pass along to just one senior, it would be to follow your dreams. Over the last few years, I've carried on an unscientific study regarding people who are truly happy with their lives – those who seem to enjoy what they do – those select few who've followed their dreams.

Arnold Palmer loves to play golf. He could have been a successful greens keeper like his father but he loved to play. Palmer once said that he couldn't believe he got paid to do what he loved. He also said recently, he'd give all the money back if he could play the way he did when he was younger. Probably one of the most famous golfers of all time, Arnold Palmer followed his dream.

Oliver Stone was drafted out of college and sent to Vietnam for a tour of duty. Rather than let it set him back, Stone used that interruption in his life to inspire the first of many great movies, *Platoon*. He went on to produce and direct *Wall Street* and *JFK*, in addition to other famous motion pictures. There was never any question what Stone wanted to do with life. He wanted to make movies. He got there by following his dreams.

Following one's dreams is not always easy. Many times you have to swim upstream against conventional wisdom. Sometimes that overnight success is ten to twelve years in the making.

Catherine Lanigan had a lifelong dream of becoming a journalist. Her family, friends, and teachers encouraged her to reach for those dreams. She was told that she could write and had the talent to make something of herself. But her life changed when she went to college. During her first semester, she was placed in a creative writing class designed for second semester seniors. It was being taught by a visiting professor from Harvard.

After submitting her first paper, the Harvard professor asked to meet with Catherine. During the meeting, he told her that her writing stunk. It was so bad, he said that he promised to pass her in the course only if she would change her major and promise never to write anything ever again.

A stunned Catherine obliged the visiting professor and held on to her other dream of graduating summa cum laude. For the next fourteen years, Catherine kept her promise to the man from Harvard and did not write. One day while attending a writers' conference with a friend, someone asked her if she was a writer. She told him that she had been told by a good authority that she had no talent. The person who asked the question, challenged Catherine to write again and when she submitted her work to him, he immediately sent it to his agent.

Catherine's dream was back on track. She had two things the Harvard professor recognized but lacked – talent and a dream. If the jealous professor had had his way, we'd never been able to read wonderful novels like *Romancing the Stone*, *Jewel of the Nile*, and *Wings of Destiny*, as well as the seventeen other works that bear the name of Catherine Lanigan.

Sure Skip, you might say, these are all famous people you're taking about. Show me just one person who lives here that has followed his dreams and become happy and successful. I can do better than that. Three come to mind immediately.

Billy Gent has always loved animals. When we were in the fourth grade at Trent Park School he was always bringing some animal to show and tell. From birds to lizards, puppies to kittens, Billy loved his animals. I even remember standing in front of the old Tryon Theater one afternoon watching Billy trying to catch pigeons from the rooftop of the lawyers' office across the street. When Billy fell off the roof, we all thought he was dead. After we graduated from high school, I went off to college and Billy took off following his dream. Today Billy Gent is the owner of several of the most successful pet shops in the area, *Bill's Pet Shop*. He got there by following his dreams.

Just over ten years ago, my friend and classmate Tommy Marsh had a successful job working in Virginia. He was making plenty of money but something was missing. He was not happy. Tommy did something most people his age would never do. He changed careers. Tommy wanted to return to his hometown and teach at his old high school. I'm sure most people who knew him thought Tommy to be a little crazy to give up his higher paying job and become a teacher. But Tommy Marsh wanted more from life. Since his return to New Bern, Tommy has happiness that he lacked before. He has also found success. Not only has he been recognized as one of the best teachers at New Bern High, he has revitalized another of his dreams. He has built New Bern High into one of the powerhouses in North Carolina in the sport of wrestling. I'll bet a dollar to a dime that Tommy Marsh would rather be called "Coach" than any other title in the world.

In April, I attended the funeral of my friend, G.E. Lee. His death left me rethinking two words; courage and attitude.

G.E. followed his father into the home building business. Unlike many people who consider joining their parents' profession, G.E. loved building houses. His love for home construction showed in his work. He was known for building a good house. Just over five and a half years ago, G.E.

was diagnosed with brain cancer. That's when I knew he loved his work.

Most people when confronted with the finality that can come with a disease like cancer take a different fork in that new road. They quit their jobs, travel more, read more and start doing something that they like. Time becomes their enemy and they want to get in every bit of living that they can.

G.E. never changed. He continued to work at the same job; building houses. Why didn't he change or quit? Why did he keep his sense of humor and his positive attitude? Because G.E. was already following his dream.

Everyone knows that success can be measured by a strong financial statement. But there is more, much more. Happiness and friends are far more important as a real bottom line. Those who follow their dreams always seem to find true happiness and friends and for some special reason, financial rewards always find them.

So to the graduating class of 2001, along with those who feel trapped on a one-way street. Don't just take it from me; there are far too many examples of people who will tell you to follow your dreams. It will make a difference.

Father's Day

June is for fathers. When I was a kid, on Father's Day Sunday they pinned a flower on us when we walked into Sunday service at church – a red one if your father was alive and a white one if he had passed away. I'm glad they don't do that any more. I'm glad that when I celebrate Father's Day it is to remember the life my dad lived and to celebrate that life.

We always remember our mothers, but often fathers are overlooked. Most of us have mental pictures of the perfect father. My generation remembers the TV show "Father Knows Best" with Jim and Margaret Anderson, Bud, Betty, and Kitten. At the end of each episode, Father always had a lesson to teach us.

What we found out was that the Anderson family, although they tried to profile the 1950s American families, left an image no one could really live up to. Reality told us that our fathers worked hard trying to give us our share of the American dream. The father of the real 50s families, those Tom Brokaw refers to as members of the "Greatest Generation," may have tried to measure up to Jim Anderson, but in many ways probably exceeded his expectations.

I still see fathers, in my mind's eye, in a warm reverent light. I see parties with daughters dancing on their daddies' feet. I see dads out in the yard, after a hard day at work, playing catch with their sons. I see him fighting back a tear as he raises the veil, places a kiss on the cheek of his best girl and passes her hand to another man who is now filling her life. And I see the beam on his face as he stands beside his son and places a ring in a preacher's hand.

My father passed away six years ago this month. It seems like he's only been gone a few weeks. I'm over the pain of missing him and now enjoy the memory of his life and the legacy that he left me – a legacy not of material things but of spiritual things. He taught me the difference between right and wrong. Dad developed in me a sense of fair play and honesty and to be thankful for my family and friends. He also showed me that in our lives that there will be sadness as well as joy and that crying is as much a part of life as laughing.

America has changed since the days of Jim Anderson. Today there are fathers who do not live at home and there are substitute ones who do. There is probably more pressure on dads today than ever. But after all is said and done all fathers love their kids. So if you're lucky enough to still have a father and missed calling him last Sunday to wish him a happy Father's Day, the good news is that it is still not too late. I can assure you, to him, it will make a difference.

The Day the Tar Heels "FINALLY" Came to Town

A major sporting event is going to explode in eastern Carolina this Saturday. No, it's not NASCAR nor is it the ACC Tournament. It's a whole lot more. You might call it the Carolina Bowl. Two football teams with a pure hatred of each other, both with losing seasons will meet for in-state bragging rights. For the first time, the Tar Heels of UNC will meet the East Carolina Pirates on their own turf, in Greenville.

From all over the state the fans will trek across the farms and through the fishing villages of the east to converge on what was once Mr. Ficklin's old tobacco field to witness the biggest sporting event ever held east of I-95.

The contest between the two schools started over thirty years ago and is one that is steeped in history. It is also cloaked in controversy, close calls, close games and petty bickering. Of the nine times the teams have played each other, Carolina has won seven of the games; ECU has won one and there was one tie. Of those games won by the Heels, four have been decided by a total of 10 points. I know because I've seen them all.

The first time the Tar Heels agreed to play the upstart eastern school was in 1972. That year Carolina won; 42 to 19. The game was played in an icy drizzle that was just one or two degrees above a snowfall. Being a Carolina grad, I made my wife Jane, who graduated from ECU, sit in Kenan Stadium until all the zeroes were on the clock. Back in the early days of the series, Jane and I had a bet. If ECU won, I'd pay her $500. If the Tar Heels won, she had to take the garbage out for the next year.

In 1973, I almost wrote the check. At halftime the Pirates were up 21 to zip. I had never seen Kenan so charged. But the Tar Heels would not be denied. With almost no time left on the clock, the Pirates had stopped a Tar Heel drive that neared the goal line. A late flag by the ACC official gave the ball back to Carolina. As I recall, it took the Tar Heels all four downs to punch it in. The Pirates lost 27 to 28.

UNC and ECU didn't play again until 1975. The night before the game, long-time ECU Athletic Director, Clarence Stasavich died. The next morning, I opened the sports section of the Raleigh paper and the half-page picture on the front page made the hair on my arms stand up. The picture showed Stas, during his coaching days, standing on the sidelines, his right hand on the shoulder of a player and his left hand pointing toward the field. The player, all American New Bern native Norman Swindell, had died during his senior year when he played for Stasavich. At that moment, I knew there would be thirteen players on the field for ECU that day. With fifteen seconds left on the clock, I wrote my first check and handed it to Jane. As she waved it high over her head, the entire ECU side burst into cheers. The Pirates had won 38 to 17.

One of the most bizarre games was held in 1976. Pat Dye's undefeated team had just received ECU's first ever top 20 national ranking and was looking ahead to a bowl game. The Tar Heels won again, depriving ECU an extra game that year. During that game, the Heels never crossed the goal line. It took the longest field goal in the history of Kenan Stadium for Carolina to win it – 12 to 10.

The next year, refusing to be beaten by an ECU team, UNC Head Coach Dick Crum elected to kick a last minute field goal to tie the Pirates. The game ended in a 24 – 24 "sister kisser" that no one cared for.

The last two games played between the Tar Heels and the Pirates were pretty much routs by Carolina with the series ending in 1981. For whatever the reason, UNC Athletic Director Bill Cobey and his predecessor, John Swofford, had no further desire to play their sister institution, stating that (1) they had nothing to gain and everything to lose and (2) that if they played

ECU, they'd be forced to play other in-state programs like Western Carolina and Appalachian.

Before long that excuse disappeared. The Pirates football program started gaining national recognition and schools like Western and ASU dropped to Division 2. Still Carolina continued to schedule national powerhouses like Bowling Green and Ohio University. I guess that's when I started moving my support to the Pirate program. Long ago my mother had taught me to treat others as I'd like to be treated. I learned that the snobbery of Swofford and Company was just poor manners. Talking down to those of us who are fierce easterners ruffled my feathers.

But it took two things to bring the schools back to the playing field: the departure of John Swofford and the North Carolina Legislature. The UNC athletic department saw the handwriting on the wall and rather than having a law like those in other states that require in-state schools to play each other, tucked their tails between their legs and scheduled a series with East Carolina.

In 2001, a new generation of college football fans, who had never seen ECU and UNC "tee it up," met in Chapel Hill for one barnburner of a game. It was one of the few times in Kenan history that fans on both sides stood up for the whole game. And as has been the rule rather than the exception, the game came down to a final tick on the clock with the Pirates limping home, just four points short of a victory.

This Saturday, both teams have losing records. But the atmosphere will be bowl like. The Tar Heels will play in the most hostile environment they've ever seen. And the Pirates will have a long time monkey on their back. For the 50,000 or so who'll be in attendance and the thousands more who'll watch on statewide TV, this game will be for all the marbles. During the last twenty years I have watched the Pirate program grow. I've missed less than five home games. I've seen the Miamis and the Florida States play in Dowdy-Flicklin. I've seen bowl invitations accepted there, but for me and, for many more like me, this is the big one. Will I wear purple or powder blue? What do you think?

Thanksgiving

One of my favorite days of the year is Thanksgiving. Unlike Christmas and the Fourth of July, Thanksgiving always falls on a weekday and people across our great land set aside that one day to feast, remember and give thanks. Sometimes the remembrances are joyful and other times painful, but at least for one day all of America stops, prays and hopes.

I remember as a kid – the special time when my family got together at my grandmother's house in Greensboro – awakening to the smells of sweet potatoes and pumpkin pie baking in her oven. Watching as my aunts set the table and helping by carrying bowls of gravy and plates of hot biscuits, anxiously awaiting the time when what I thought was the biggest chicken I'd ever seen eased from the oven, hoping for one of the huge drumsticks.

Christmas is celebrated by hundreds of songs but only three come to mind for Thanksgiving, some not even heard today. Songs like "Over the River and Through the Woods," "There's No Place Like Home for the Holidays" (sung only by Perry Como), and of course the traditional classic, "We Gather Together" – a song I'm told the Pilgrims sang.

After lunch the women -- my mom and grandmother along with a company of aunts and older cousins -- cleared the table and retreated to the kitchen for what I was told was called "women's talk." The men staked out chairs and couches in front of the black and white TV to watch what has become a modern Thanksgiving tradition, football. Shortly however, the TV played to a blank audience. The room seemed to expand and withdraw like a Disney cartoon, the snoring covering the sound of the television. I have recently been told by Tony Joyner, the associate pastor at Garber Methodist Church, that the reason that this phenomena exists is that there is some sort of sedative produced in a man's body when huge amounts of turkey are consumed. Maybe that explains why the phenomenon continues today.

While the adults talked and slept, the rest of us went into the yard to play. For some reason one of the cousins always brought an old football and we chose sides for a game of touch football. I always wanted to play on my cousin Judy's team. She was the best passer in the "Thanksgiving" league and it was fun to be on the team with a girl quarterback when we won.

In those days, Thanksgiving kicked off the Christmas season. The following Friday was usually the biggest shopping day of the year. Over the years, however, things have really changed. Now the Christmas season seems to get started the day after Halloween.

It was a no-no in our house to put up a tree before Thanksgiving, yet today I've seen trees up in stores as early as November first. I realize that the shopping season fuels our economy, but I don't want to see the special day we call Thanksgiving become absorbed into the madness.

Most people don't know this, but only two countries in the world legally set aside a day to give thanks to a Supreme Being. Those countries are Canada and the United States of America.

I hope when you and your family sit down this year, you'll thank the One you pray to for the kindness that has been given to you, and I especially hope you will be thankful to live in a country that sets a day aside to give you that opportunity.

Thanksgiving makes a difference in my life and I hope in yours. One of my prayers this year is that its true meaning is never forgotten because of the holiday season. Happy Thanksgiving.

Field of Diamonds

I'm sure that the worst part of my day is getting up in the morning. The odd thing is that it doesn't matter what time it is, getting out of bed is tough. I think that I could sleep twelve to fourteen hours and still hate getting out of bed.

I know a lot of people who seem to really enjoy the morning hours. As I sleepwalk to let the cat out at six in the morning, I'm amazed by the traffic that I see on the golf course at that time of day. Joggers and walkers are all over the place. As I make my way back to my bed, I look at my watch and say to myself, only an hour and a half more left.

My friend Bill Brinkley loves getting up in the morning. He arises at 5:30each day, no matter what time he goes to bed the night before. He says that it allows him to ease into his day. He reads the newspaper, checks the TV for news, weather and sports and still has time to meet the guys at Pete and Nikki's for breakfast. I just can't do that. I'd rather be bagging a few more Z's.

The good thing about waking up being the worst part of the day is that from there on out, everything else is downhill. That leads me to the best part of my day. After the coffee is started and the cobwebs swept from my eyes, I harness my two dogs and set out for our morning walk on the golf course. By the time Thumper, Little Mutt and I reach the first fairway, we're joined by my two cats, Bob and Mister.

It is the only part of my day that is quiet and peaceful. It is my time to commune with God and to thank Him for all the wonderful blessings He has bestowed on my family and me. It is the time of day that I talk to myself. Those 20 minutes are what starts my day off and I don't care if it's raining, 17 degrees or a perfect October day. It is my time of day.

The other day I was finishing my walk on a frosted golf course. As the sun rose, its rays began filtering through the frozen grass. The effect was making the grass sparkle. Unlike a mirage which disappears before you can get to it, the sparkling grass was everywhere, even right under my feet.

My wife, Jane, is dazzled by anything that sparkles. When we go to New York and walk through the diamond district, she is drawn to a jewelry store window like mosquitoes to a yellow light bulb. If I lose her on the sidewalk, all I have to do is look for a window sparkling with diamonds, and I'll find her.

Like Jane in New York, I was dazzled that day as the sun rose on the golf course. All around me I saw sparkling objects shining in the brilliant morning sun.

As I stood in the middle of the first fairway, captured by nature's brilliance, I noticed a lone figure approaching me. Rather than using the cart paths, like most walkers and joggers do, this person was walking on the grass. As the person got closer, I recognized him. It was Bob Clement. When Bob got to me he stopped and asked, "Can you believe the golf course this morning?"

When I acknowledged that I was enjoying the sight as well, Bob said, "Skip, I know it's cold outside and a lot of people would rather use a treadmill or a Nordic track, but you can't get this inside."

I agreed with Bob then he continued his walk. As he left, he called back over his shoulder and said, "It's like we're walking in a field of diamonds."

Bob, I couldn't have said it better. Even if getting up is the worse part of your day, a good walk outside in the morning can really make a difference.

Norman Swindell

With a major league baseball strike looming, I couldn't be happier. It's football season. As far as I'm concerned the rich crybaby players of baseball can strike themselves out of existence, then maybe we can have football all year long.

My first real interest in football came when my father took me to Kafer Park to see New Bern High School play. The coach then was a guy by the name of Joe Caruso. Coach Caruso took a couple of his teams to the state playoffs, but to me he was more famous for coaching some of the guys I grew up looking up to, people like Norman Kellum, Ken Morris, and the Clement twins. Caruso was so popular that the stadium at the new high school bears his name.

When I made it to high school, I was privileged to be the manager for our new coach, Bill Klutz. Don't let the name fool you, he was far from a fumbler. Coach Klutz replaced coach Arbs, who left after a series of losing years. Klutz brought with him the most beautiful offense I have ever seen – the Single Wing. Prior to Coach Klutz, the Bears played a "T" formation. The "T" had a quarterback who lined up directly under the center. A fullback lined up behind the quarterback and left and right halfbacks flanked to either side, thus forming the imaginary "T."

The Single Wing was a thing of pure beauty. First it had an unbalanced line. The center, for those few who don't know what he does, is the guy that hikes the ball. This guy did not line up in the center, that position belonged to a guard. In the back field only the fullback remained. Gone were the halfbacks, who were replaced by the wingback and the blocking back. The tailback, who replaced the quarterback, took the snap on the run – kind of like the present shotgun – instead of from under center.

The one thing that Coach Arbs left Coach Klutz was a full stable of running backs, people like Cliffie Rowe, Don Davis, Ronald "Crazy Legs" Wallace and my favorite, Norman Swindell. The two years those guys played for Klutz were his best, and we won the conference.

Over at ECU, a guy by the name of Clarence Stasavich brought the Single Wing to the college level. New Bern became a perfect recruiting ground. While Don Davis went to Wake Forest, Norman Swindell found a perfect home with Coach Stasavich and started his sophomore year on defense. That year, 1963, Wake Forest agreed to come to ECU for the dedication of the new Ficklin Stadium. Lining up against his best friend Davis, Swindell could not have been happier. That evening Davis and another well-known offensive back by the name of Brian Piccolo (remember the movie "Brian's Song") spent most of the game on their backsides, thanks to Norman Swindell. ECU won the game, 20 to 10.

The next year Swindell was moved to the offense and fit in perfectly at his old position of blocking back. The year was his best and the best of Stasavich's tenure. The Pirates were selected to go to a bowl in January, but Swindell would never make the trip. He died in a hunting accident in December. I'll never forget seeing coach Stas as we searched South River for Norman's body. He stood on the beach with the others, his trademark "pulled back" hair blowing in the Northeast breeze, a tear tickling down his cheek.

On Friday, Oct. 24, 1975, Clarence Stasavich died. He had long since left as the Pirate head football coach and joined the legendary chancellor Leo Jenkins, as his athletic director. Together they laid the groundwork for the promising future that would follow their legacy, but still in 1975 the Pirates had something to prove. The day after Stas died ECU met arch nemesis UNC in Chapel Hill, as usual, very much the underdog. That Saturday morning prior to the game I opened the *News and Observer* and turned to the sports page. Across the bottom of the page were the following words: "East Carolina Mourns its Fallen Leader." Above the inscription was a half page photograph. The picture showed a younger Stasavich with his hand on the shoulder of a football player, pointing toward the football field. I handed the paper to my wife Jane and said, "You better count on a win today, there's no way our 11 can beat your 13." The other person in the picture was Norman Swindell. That Saturday, the Pirates played a flawless game and won, 38 to 17.

I guess that's why I love college football so much. It's more than a game. It's the stories, it's a mascot called Reveille, a fiery spear in the center of the field that starts a game. It's winning one for the Gipper, or the number of a fallen player sewn on a jersey. It's the attitude of "any given Saturday," but most of all it's tradition.

A few years ago, Norman Swindell took his place in the ECU Hall of Fame, along side his famous coach. I am troubled that he has never been selected for the same honor at his high school. Maybe this year those at New Bern High will make a difference and include Norman in that special group.

* * *

What a wonderful coincidence: As my article is going to press, I have just been notified by Steve Bengel that the New Bern High School Hall of Fame committee has just selected Norman as a 2002 inductee. Sleep well my friend.

Reflections – The Promise of a New Year

The first of the year is a time for making promises. For most people it is time for resolutions. I'm going to lose weight, or get into shape, or work smarter. All are fine but most are forgotten long before the end of February.

For me, I've tried all the resolutions, so I don't try to fool myself by making promises I have no intention of keeping. There is one thing, however that the first of the year provides and that is a reflection of the year gone by. These are some of the things that made the year 2000 unique, not only to those of us fortunate to live in Trent Woods but to those of us fortunate to be Americans.

Probably the biggest story of the year was the Presidential election. For over a month most of us woke up each morning asking the same question, "Who's going to be the next President?" For me the important issue is not who won or how it happened, but what did not happen. The winner was not thrust into office because of his association with the military, there were no tanks in our streets, and there were no angry masses on the Washington Mall shouting at each other. As frustrating as it seemed, most Americans just sat back and let the system work.

As for local politics, my hat is off to the Mayor and the commissioners of our fine town. Theirs is a thankless job. As best I can tell, no one is using his or her position as a stepping-stone to national prominence. No, they are just giving of their time to help run a small southern town.

I'm thankful that we didn't have a hurricane this past year. And speaking of the weather, there could not have been a better place to live in all these United States than Trent Woods during the month of October – warm days and cool nights, all the golf, boating and just sitting outside anyone could want.

Although an early snowfall postponed our second annual Christmas parade, it was not canceled and was even more successful than the one the previous year. There could not have been a better choice for Grand Marshall than former mayor George Scott, the unofficial "father" of Trent Woods.

Locally, the year 2000 brought the beginning of the multi-million dollar project that Tryon Palace has started at the old Barbour Boats Works property. When it is finished, I am told that it will be a family-oriented attraction that will bring in people from all over America.

We also saw the completion of the new Riverfront Civic Center. This new building has already become a tremendous asset to our community and will continue to be one for years to come.

All in all, the year 2000 has left a favorable memory on most of us. It started with a worldwide bang and ended as most years do with some happiness, some sadness, but most of all change. I hope the changes were good for all of you and that they made a difference.

The Trent River

The Trent River has always played a major roll in the life of Trent Woods. In fact our town is named after the river. Growing up in Trent Woods, the river was the focal point of summer.

On a typical summer day when I was fifteen, I would mow a few yards in the morning so I could have enough money to fill up two six gallon pressurized tanks with gas and oil and head for Kimbrell's Outboard Service where the "Bat" boat was docked. The "Bat" boat was a 15-foot 8 inch Sabre. For some reason in 1961, the eight inches was important in describing a boat's length.

Originally she was pink and had a 35 horse Johnson on the back but the year before I had painted her navy blue and re-powered her with an Evinrude 60. She sported a white racing stripe on her bow and had large rear fins, reminiscent of a De Soto automobile. My friends dubbed her the "Bat" boat, in honor of "Batman."

On most days, Dale Goldman would meet me and we'd leave Lawson Creek and head upriver. The action was at the Trent Pines and New Bern Golf and County Club. That's where the girls were.

Usually, we'd stop near the Jaycee Park and listen for Paul Johnson. Paul had a racing utility which was one of the smallest boats on the river. It may have been small but it was by far the loudest. Generally we could hear Paul long before we could see him. Upon confirming that Paul was somewhere on the river, we'd proceed to the Trent Pines Club.

The Trent Pines Club had the first real swimming pool I had ever seen, except in the movies. It was also home to summer water ski shows and boat races. But most of all, at least to a bunch of teenage boys, that's where the girls were and they all wanted to go water skiing. It was a real joy having a boat.

After spending the morning at Trent Pines, we'd move to the country club. "The Club" as we called it didn't have a swimming pool at that time but it did have a great dock with a dock house and high dive and, oh yeah, more girls who wanted to go skiing. Have I mentioned what a joy it was having a boat?

Of course, the competition was great. It seemed that all my friends had boats too. Bill Ramsey had a Century inboard speedboat. It was 18-feet of gorgeous mahogany. Sonny Roberts had a little brown boat that when fully loaded the following wake would almost swamp it – unless the riders all moved to the bow.

Jim Bryan's boat was the best wake jumper. His 16-foot Matthews, built right here in Trent Woods, would become completely airborne when crossing the wake of a larger boat.

The fastest boat on the river belonged to Frankie Spruill. He had a Yellow Jacket 16-footer with a Mercury "Mark 78-A" on the back. This little rocket ship could reach speeds of more than 40 miles an hour. Even the Wildlife guys couldn't catch him.

With all the boat traffic, most people might think that things could get dangerous but I remember few accidents ever taking place. Oh, there was the time that David Patterson failed to turn quickly enough when slinging a skier to the beach at the club and ended up, boat and all, on the eighteenth green (they say Jack Lee never flinched and made his putt). And, there was the time that Bob Davis fell out of his duck boat. As he fell, he turned the motor so that the boat went into circles. All we could do is wait an hour or so until it ran out of gas. These incidents were few and I never remember anyone getting seriously hurt.

After a day of water skiing, diving off the power lines that crossed the river and trying to get a couple of girls to go with us to "Wall Creek," Dale and I would head back down the river to Lawson Creek. We'd smile at each other knowing that we lived in the best place on earth. Growing up on the Trent River, has really made a difference in my life.

Wonder How that Happened?
A short, short story

When I was growing up, things were, well, pretty much defined. Right was right, left was left, up was up, and down was down. I learned colors before I was in the first grade. I knew that a ripe lemon was yellow and a ripe orange was orange.

Lately, however, I've noticed that things aren't so well defined. Sometimes I think George Orwell was right. What used to be a given is not anymore. For instance, during my travels, especially on the interstates, I've seen a trucking company called "Yellow" freight lines. The trucks are painted a bright orange with the words "Yellow" lettered on the side.

One day about a year ago while traveling Interstate 95 I pulled into a truck stop to get gas. While filling up I saw a "Yellow" freight truck sitting in the parking lot.

When I went in to pay for my gas, the restaurant area was full. On one side, a group of truckers was gathered together having lunch and on the other a group of bikers, on their way back from the annual trek to Myrtle Beach, were doing the same.

I told myself that if I were ever going to find out why "Yellow" trucks were painted orange, this was going to be my best opportunity. "Who's driving the Yellow truck?" I shouted out over the crowded room. A burly fellow wearing a black hat with number three embroidered on it called back and said, "Who wants to know?"

"I do," I said. "I want to know why the name on your truck says 'Yellow' but the paint job is orange."

The truck driver stood up and walked over to me. By that time the room had hushed and all eyes were on us.

"It's not orange," he said. "It's yellow."

"No, you're wrong," I stood my ground. "Any first grader knows that yellow is the color of a lemon. Your truck is the color of an orange."

"If I say it's yellow, then it's yellow." The trucker moved toward me as I backed toward the door.

"The dude's right," a voice behind me said. "Your truck is orange not yellow."

"Do what?" the truck driver turned to the biker who'd defended me. "You calling me a liar."

"Yeah, you 300-pound piece of blubber. And your mama too."

With that, twenty truckers and twenty bikers leapt to their feet. When I slipped out the front door, the restaurant was full of noise as insults were followed by fists, chairs and flying food.

As I turned my car onto the interstate ramp I said to myself, "Wow, wonder how all that got started."

About the Author

Skip Crayton is a lifelong resident of New Bern, a small town in coastal North Carolina, located where the Trent River flows into the Neuse River, the widest river in America. An avid sailor, his love for the river is only exceeded by his passion for writing.

Upon graduating from New Bern High School, Skip entered the University of North Carolina at Chapel Hill where he earned a Bachelor of Arts degree. After graduating from college, he married his high school sweetheart, Jane Cox, and then headed off for a short tour of duty in the United States Navy, where he learned to fly. With his military obligation complete, Skip joined his father in the family construction and land development business. Today he is an active Realtor with Coldwell Banker Willis-Smith.

He started writing seriously in 1991. Over the last thirteen years, Skip has written one journal, two novels, and two short stories. His latest book, a love story titled *The Letter Sweater*, is now in the hands of his agent, who is actively seeking publication.

In 1998, he was asked to write a column for *The Trent Woods Times*, a monthly published in his community. The success of that column led to a contract with his local newspaper, the *Sun Journal*, a daily with a circulation of over twenty-thousand.

Skip and Jane have been married for thirty-six years and have no children. They share their home with two Pekingese dogs, "Thumper" and "Little Mutt," and two cats, "Mister" and "Bob."

What people are saying about Skip Crayton and

Remember When.

"There's a writer in all of us, or at least, a story begging to be told. Trent Woods resident, Skip Crayton, has more stories than most, and as a local columnist and author, his stories emerge as effortlessly as bubbles from champagne."

> \- Linda Staunch
> Host of *Around Town*, WFXI –TV Fox– 8 and 14

*

"Simply Awesome."

> \- Colleen Maloney, Morning Anchor, WCTI-TV12

*

"I'm changing the title from 'A Collection of articles from <u>one</u> of New Bern's most popular columnists' to 'A Collection of articles from New Bern's <u>most</u> popular columnist'"

> \- Lockwood Phillips, Host of *Viewpoints*. WTKF 107.3 The Talk FM

*

"Skip Crayton recalls the fun and freedom of growing up in New Bern during the 1950's and '60s."

> \- *Our State*, North Carolina

Quick **Order Form**

Telephone Orders: 252-638-8094
                   Toll Free 1-877-830-0759

Email orders: crayton@cox.net

Online orders: www.skipcrayton.com

Postal Orders: McBryde Publishing
                   108 Dogwood Lane
                   New Bern, NC 28562

ORDER FORM

Name _____

Address_____

City_____State_____Zip_____

Telephone_____

Email_____

_____ Copies of *Remember When* at $14.95 each
            PLUS $3.95 Shipping and Handling

We accept Check, Visa, and MasterCard

Card Number_____

Name on Card_____

Expiration Date_____

NC Residents at 7% Sales Tax